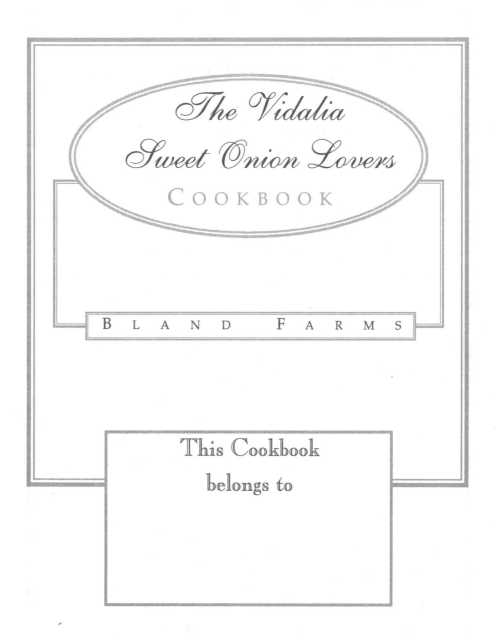

The Vidalia
Sweet Onion Lovers
C O O K B O O K

B L A N D F A R M S

This Cookbook
belongs to

Bland Farms

Home of the World Famous
Vidalia Sweet Onion

1-800-VIDALIA
1-800-843-2542

Copyright © 1996, Bland Farms
P.O. Box 506-630 • Glennville, Georgia 30427

First Printing   April, 1996
Second Printing   April, 1997
Third Printing   April, 1998

Cover Photo:
      Photographer: Joseph Byrd
      Stylist: Susan Lynah
      Props: Cobb's Galleries, Inc. •   Savannah, Georgia
                Sir Billy's Cottage •   Richmond Hill, Georgia
      Recipe: Whole Vidalias with Sweet Pea Dressing (pg. 82)

Cover Design: Georgia Byrd

Library of Congress Catalog Card Number 96-96431

IBSN 0-9652480-0-3

Printed in the United States of America

TOOF COOKBOOK DIVISION

STARR★TOOF

670 South Cooper Street
Memphis, TN 38104

Table of Contents

The Bland Farms History.............................5

Appetizers & Hors d'Oeuvres 9

Breads & Loaves 19

Salads & Salad Dressings 23

Soups & Sandwiches 45

Baked & Stuffed Treats 63

Casseroles & Souffles 79

Vegetables & Stir Fries 105

Meat, Chicken & Seafood 127

Pies, Quiche & Omelets...........................145

Pickles, Relishes & Sauces 159

Special Vidalia Sweet Onion Treats 171

Indexes 191

B L A N D   F A R M S

A Dedication

Forty years ago, the dream of Bland Farms began with two beautiful people, whose love for the rich Southern land was almost as intense as their love for each other. Together they set out to forge a legacy, that over the years has become known as Bland Farms, The Home of The World Famous Vidalia Sweet Onion! Today the farm ships these beautiful, delicious onions far and wide.

This great Southern heritage and our love of these onions have inspired us to compile this cookbook of treasured Vidalia Sweet Onion recipes. It also gives us a great deal of pleasure to dedicate this recipe collection to our founders, Raymond and Rubye Jean Bland, without whose love for one another, for God, and for the land that provides this marvel of Mother Nature, this cookbook, and indeed the reality of Bland Farms, would have been merely an unfulfilled dream!

We also dedicate this cookbook to all the Vidalia Sweet Onion lovers. It is our hope that you will enjoy this collection as much as we have enjoyed compiling it.

The History of Bland Farms

Researched and compiled by David Walsh

For many, the Bland Farms name has come to represent quality products provided by an efficient company. For others, Bland Farms is that pleasant mail-order business with friendly people answering the easy-to-remember 1-800-VIDALIA number. However, for those who truly know the company, and the people who make up that company, Bland Farms is much, much more.

Bland Farms – The Beginning

The history of Bland Farms goes back more than 50 years to the 1940's when a young man named Raymond Bland, then 18 years old, began a small 50-acre farm by planting patches of tobacco and peanuts. Raymond, who had grown up on his father's farm, had already cultivated a deep love for both farming and managing a farm.

But the real love of Raymond's life did not become a part of the Bland family until 1948 when Raymond married Rubye Jean Bradley. From that day on, Mr. Raymond and Miss Rubye Jean (now affectionately called "Momma Jean") have worked side-by-side to both raise a family and raise the crops that have made Bland Farms a household name.

In 1950, the couple moved to a 50-acre farm five miles away from the Bland homestead. The farm, located on a winding dirt road, was a run-down place that possessed few creature comforts but was beautifully draped with large pecan trees. For several years the Blands worked feverishly to improve the land and produce good crops.

Raymond and Rubye Jean were blessed with good years, and by 1954 their efforts with tobacco, corn and hogs helped them build a modern home for the growing Bland family, which now included 2 girls, Shirley and Hollie. Within the next two years the farm grew by 50 acres when Mr. Raymond & Mrs. Rubye Jean bought land from a neighbor. They also made an advance in their farm equipment with the purchase of a two-row tractor to speed the farming operation. In the fall of 1956, the Bland's only son, Delbert, was born. Five years later, the last of the Bland children, Faye, was born. As the children grew, they worked side-by-side on the farm, helping with the planting, the feeding of the livestock and the harvesting of the crops. When Mr. Raymond began growing tomatoes for market, the entire family spent many hours in the packing shed grading and shipping tomatoes to distant markets.

The family, under the strong leadership and love of Mr. Raymond and Mrs. Rubye Jean, worked tirelessly and was blessed with many good harvests. As a result, the farm grew.

During the late '50s and '60s, as the Bland operations prospered, Delbert was there, watching as the tractor-trailers carted produce to market. He was fascinated with the idea of the Bland products going to distant places. As Delbert grew and graduated from high school, he knew this fascination would play an important role in his future and in the future of Bland Farms.

It was in a crop that the Blands had not yet grown that Delbert's dream would be realized. That crop was, of course, the Vidalia Sweet Onion.

Those Very Special Onions

Vidalia Sweet Onions, which are such an important part of Bland Farms and the agricultural community of southeast Georgia, began their rise to fame more than 60 years ago. In 1931, a farmer in Vidalia, Georgia, by the name of Moses Coleman, planted some onions that proved, once harvested, to be unexpectedly sweet! For many in the southeast Georgia area, this discovery proved to be a major boost that helped their farms survive through the Depression years.

Word of these incredibly sweet onions spread and in the 1950s and 1960s, both production and demand for the Vidalia Sweets grew at a slow, but steady, pace. By the mid 1970s, 600 acres of onions were in cultivation. Today, more than 12,000 acres of Vidalia Sweet Onions are being grown with Bland Farms accounting for almost 2000 of those acres.

As fame of these delicious onions grew, farmers sought to preserve the uniqueness of this crop by acquiring legal status. In 1986, Georgia's state legislature did just that by limiting the growing area of the onions to 20 southeast Georgia counties. In 1989, the Vidalias gained federal recognition and protection through the Federal Marketing Order No. 955. This order makes the selling of non-Vidalia Sweet Onions as Vidalias illegal.

Bland Farms & The Vidalia Sweet Onion

Once Delbert graduated from high school, he devoted his full attention to the task of running a farm, and together with Mr. Raymond, decided to enter the Vidalia Sweet Onion business. Their first year with the delicate onions proved to be a complete disaster. The harvest was miserable and the profits were nonexistent. Instead of quitting, however, they tried again. In 1976, their persistance paid off and after a bountiful crop, Bland Farms was in the onion business.

But producing a good onion crop was not enough. Delbert's dream went beyond the art of farming. Delbert's dream included seeing his family's products grow from a regional specialty to a national (and international) necessity. To accomplish this, a network of contacts and customers were needed where none had existed before. Many of those who became privy to Delbert's ideas viewed his aspirations as unreasonable, excessive, and to a few, insane. But Delbert was undaunted. To sell his onions, Delbert began traveling to all parts of the country, meeting people, handing out onions and winning friends with his simple country charm, his quick wit and straightforward honesty. From these initial contacts, the Bland Farms mail order business gained its beginnings. With an aggressive advertising program and products that sell themselves, Bland Farms quickly became a mail order powerhouse in the fresh produce industry.

Shortly after the creation of the mail order business, Bland Farms gained another valuable asset to assist with this operation, namely Delbert's wife, Sandra Brewton Bland. Those who know Delbert will quickly recognize that one of his greatest strengths is his ability to surround himself with exceptional people who share his vision and enthusiastically put their hearts to the task. In his wife, he has found far more than a loving mother to his children, Landis, Troy and Courtney, he has also found an extraordinarily capable business partner who has taken over the mail order division. Under her direction, Sandra has turned the mail order division into one of the most productive branches of the farm through her combination of impressive organizational skills and her warm and loving spirit. Sandra has expanded the mail order offerings beyond the initial fresh produce into all types of farm-fresh products including relishes and dressings, cakes and pies and even gourmet popcorn.

In 1995, Bland Farms made another major decision...the decision to enter into the frozen food market with the introduction of their "Vidalia O's"® frozen onion rings and "Vidalia Bits"® diced onion pieces. By utilizing the existing contacts and marketing structures already in place in the wholesale and mail order division, the "O's" and

"Bits" have quickly earned a special place in the hearts of onion lovers across the country.

Anytime a business grows, the number of employees also grows. In the early years of the mail order business, a handful of people hired on a seasonal basis were sufficient to meet the demand for the sweet onions. However, as word of those fantastic onions spread, the demand snowballed and soon, permanent employees were needed. To fill that need, Mr. Raymond and Delbert didn't need to look far. With Mr. Raymond's and Mrs. Rubye Jean's large families, willing and capable workers were just a few miles away. Today, Bland Farms proudly employs many members of the extended Bland family. Call the toll-free 1-800-VIDALIA number and you may find yourself talking to Mr. Raymond's sister, Katie Lee; or Mrs. Rubye Jean's sister-in-law, Laverne. Granddaughter Kristie serves as Sandra's very efficient secretary. Cousin Dean is Mr. Raymond's right-hand man in the field. Sandra's mother, Momma Dee, fills in wherever she is needed most. And the list goes on and on.

Bland Farms, with its reputation for providing a family-like working atmosphere, has attracted many others in the community. Visitors to the farm have frequently commented on the warm atmosphere.

One of the greatest testimonials to the legacy of Bland Farms, as created by Mr. Raymond and Mrs. Rubye Jean, is the incredibly strong sense of family that is maintained in all aspects of the operations. Teamwork, mutual benefit and mutual respect are all indelible themes that run through every action, every decision and every word. In their relationship with their customers, the Bland family has demanded that each customer be treated and thought of as being an integral member of the Bland Farms family. The smallest concern voiced by a customer is carefully scrutinized and responded to. The slightest hint of dissatisfaction is met with an unquestioning willingness to please. And a compliment from a customer is valued as much as a son values a word-of-praise from his father.

Bland Farms has changed greatly in the past 50 years, but Mr. Raymond and Mrs. Rubye Jean have made sure that some things never change: their love for one another and their family; their love of God and commitment to their church; their love of the land and their pride in their products; and their desire to serve their community and their customers by giving their very best.

Appetizers
&
Hors d'Oeuvres

BLAND FARMS

ARMS ROLL UPS

12	slices dried beef	12	Baby Vidalia Sweet Onions
1	8-ounce package cream cheese		Salt and pepper

Lay beef out and spread cream cheese on each slice lengthwise. Place a Baby Vidalia Sweet Onion on each slice of beef and roll meat around it. This makes a nice snack or appetizer. Salt and pepper to taste. Keep refrigerated.
Makes 12 roll ups.

Norma Arms
Allegan, MI

BERT'S ZESTY VIDALIA ONION DIP

5th Place Winner Georgia National Fair

½	cup sour cream	½	teaspoon prepared mustard
½	cup mayonnaise or salad dressing	⅓	cup chopped Vidalia Sweet Onion
1	tablespoon snipped chives	1	teaspoon curry powder
1	teaspoon Worcestershire sauce		

Blend sour cream and mayonnaise. Add remaining ingredients; mix well. Cover. Refrigerate at least one hour before serving.

Bert Hawley
Warner Robins, GA

CASSIE'S VIDALIA CRACKER APPETIZER

4	cups crushed saltine crackers	3	cups scalded milk
1	cup melted butter	3	eggs, beaten
½	teaspoon curry powder	1	teaspoon salt
2	cups chopped and lightly salted Vidalia Sweet Onions		Dash of pepper Parmesan cheese
1½	cups grated Cheddar cheese		Paprika
½	cup chopped fresh basil		

Combine crackers with melted butter and curry powder. Line an 11x16-inch pan with ¾ of cracker mixture. Place onions on top of cracker mixture and cover with grated Cheddar cheese. Sprinkle fresh basil on top. Combine milk, egg, salt and pepper. Pour over ingredients in pan. Sprinkle on balance of crackers. Top with light layer of Parmesan cheese and paprika. Bake 25 minutes at 375 degrees. Cut into 2-inch squares. Makes 40 squares.

Cassie Gill
Birmingham, MI

COCKTAIL DIP GUACAMOLE

2	well ripened avocados, mash in flat bottomed bowl with potato masher	2	medium-sized Vidalia Sweet Onions, chopped
4	tablespoons salsa (medium hot or to taste)	1	clove garlic, mashed Salt to taste Large firm tomato

Mix avocados, salsa and onions together. Add seasonings and place in serving bowl. Cut tomato in half and remove seeds and juice. Coarsely chop and drain well. Place tomato on top of avocado mix covering top well. Serve with corn chips of your choice. Dip through all layers to eat. Yield: 6 servings.

Dr. Arnold J. Kremen
Minneapolis, MN

DEVILED VIDALIA SWEET ONIONS

3	medium Vidalia Sweet Onions	1	4½-ounce can deviled ham
2	tablespoons chopped celery	2	tablespoons water
1	tablespoons butter or margarine	¼	cup grated Parmesan cheese
1	cup herbed dried stuffing mix		

Preheat oven to 350 degrees. Peel onions and parboil for 10 minutes. Slice in half horizontally and hollow out centers, leaving an inch rim. In a small frying pan, sauté chopped celery in butter. Combine with stuffing mix, deviled ham and water. Place onions in 1½-quart baking dish. Fill onion hollows with deviled ham mixture. Sprinkle with cheese and bake for 20 to 30 minutes until heated through. Serves 6.
Tip: Don't throw away the onion centers. Chop them and use in soup, meatloaf, salads. Sometimes add a little of the chopped centers to the dressing and ham mix.

"Vidalia Sweet Onions make this recipe SPECIAL. I made it for years before I knew about Vidalias."

Edna Anderson
Sidney, NE

FRIED VIDALIA SWEET ONION RINGS

1½	cups all-purpose flour	3	large Vidalia Sweet Onions
1½	cups beer (active or flat or at room temperature)	3	to 4 cups cooking oil

Combine flour and beer in a large bowl and blend thoroughly, using a whisk. Cover the bowl and allow the batter to set at room temperature for no less than 3 hours. Twenty minutes before the batter is ready, preheat oven to 200 degrees. Place brown paper bags or layers of paper towels on cookie sheet. Carefully peel the skins from the onions so that you do not cut into the outside onion layer. Cut onions into ¼-inch thick slices. Separate into rings. Pour oil into deep fryer or large pan and heat to 375 degrees. Dip rings into batter, fry to golden brown. Transfer to paper lined cookie sheet. To keep warm, place in oven until all onions have been fried.

Mrs. Don Sparks
Lakeland, FL

HORS D'OEUVRE

Vidalia Sweet Onions   **Crusty Italian bread**
Olive oil

Saute onions in a small amount of olive oil. Serve on a piece of Italian bread. Make as many as you want. Serve immediately. Try it, you'll love it!

" Easterners even serve fried Vidalias with crackers for cocktail time. Delicious! "

Mary V. Russo
Rutherford, NJ

HORS D'OEUVRES FOR COCKTAILS

Thinly sliced white bread   **Vidalia Sweet Onions**
Mayonnaise   **Chopped parsley**

Spread bread with mayonnaise. Slice onions into thin slices, place on bread then cover bread to make sandwiches. Using a small round cookie cutter make sandwiches into tiny rounds. Spread edges of rounds with mayonnaise and roll in chopped parsley. This will make the edges a decorative green.

" These are MOST popular with our guests and too many are hardly enough! "

Mrs. Joel A. Rogers
Wickenburg, AZ

MICROWAVED VIDALIA SWEET ONIONS

Vidalia Sweet Onions, one
    per serving
Salt
Pepper

Grated Parmesan or Romano
    cheese
Butter

Peel onions. Cut into fourths, being careful not to cut all the way through the onion. Place each onion on a square of plastic wrap. Sprinkle with salt, pepper, and grated cheese and top with a pat of butter. Wrap tightly. Microwave on high 7 to 8 minutes, depending on size of onions.

Dorothy S. Barnes
Albuquerque, NM

VIDALIA SWEET ONION APPETIZER SQUARES

1   8-ounce package cream
      cheese, softened
1 to 2 tablespoons mayonnaise
    Worcestershire sauce

Tabasco sauce
2   large Vidalia Sweet Onions,
      coarsely chopped

Blend cream cheese with mayonnaise, Worcestershire and Tabasco sauce. Stir in onions and spread on squares of oven dried toast that has had the crust removed. Top with grated Parmesan cheese. Broil. Watch carefully until browned. Remove from broiler and cut into triangles. Serve hot.

Lucy M. Hudock
Riverside, CT

VIDALIA SWEET ONION TARTS

Toast rounds
Vidalia Sweet Onions, chopped

Parmesan cheese
Mayonnaise

Cut bread into rounds and toast on one side. Mix chopped onions and mayonnaise together until spreading consistency. Add Parmesan cheese and spread on toast rounds. Place under broiler a few minutes or until bubbly. Serve immediately.

"Delicious and easy!! You can make as many as you want. There are no specific measurements. Nobody can figure out what's in them!"

Mrs. James Raye Toombs
Hawthorne, NJ

STROHM VIDALIA SWEET ONION RINGS

Vidalia Sweet Onions, one
    per serving
Milk

All-purpose flour
Salt

Slice cleaned onion approximately ⅛-inch thick. Soak in cold milk. Coat evenly with flour and french fry quickly in hot oil. Drain and serve immediately. Salt to taste.
Note: For additional variety, season flour with Mexican or Cajun seasonings.

Terry Strohm
Woodstock, IL

VIDALIA SWEET ONION APPETIZER

1   cup finely chopped Vidalia   1   cup shredded Swiss cheese
      Sweet Onions   1   cup mayonnaise

Mix all ingredients together and pour into pie plate. Bake 20 to 30 minutes at 375 to 400 degrees until brown and bubbly on top. Remove from oven and serve with your favorite crackers or bread thins.

Note: This recipe can be halved or doubled. Just keep the proportions equal.

Joyce Cekander
Olympia Fields, IL

VIDALIA SWEET ONION HORS D'OEUVRE

6   large Vidalia Sweet Onions   ½   cup water
½   cup vinegar   ½   cup mayonnaise
½   cup sugar   Celery seed, to taste

Cut onions into thin slices and marinate in vinegar, sugar, and water overnight. Drain; pat dry. Mix with mayonnaise and celery seed. Serve on melba toast rounds or crackers. Yield: 8 to 10 servings.

Note: Can also be put on top of softened cream cheese and served as cocktail spread.

Jacquelyne P. Long
Newark, DE

VIDALIA SWEET ONION SURPRISE

1   large Vidalia Sweet Onion,   1½   cups grated sharp Cheddar
      coarsely chopped   cheese, divided
1   cup mayonnaise

Mix onion, mayonnaise and 1 cup of Cheddar cheese together and pour into a 10-inch quiche dish or pie plate. Top with remaining ½ cup cheese. Bake at 350 degrees for 20 to 25 minutes. Serve as hot before-dinner appetizer with salted crackers. Serves 6-8

Mrs. Milo Van Voris
Tucson, AZ

VIDALIA SWEET ONION WITH CREAMY OLIVE DIP APPETIZER

1	Vidalia Sweet Onion flower	¼	teaspoon dill
1	cup sour cream	2	tablespoons finely minced
¼	cup mayonnaise		stuffed olives
1	teaspoon Worcestershire sauce		

Combine sour cream and mayonnaise. Add remaining ingredients and blend well. Serve with Onion Flower for dipping.

Vidalia sweet onion flower: Peel a large Vidalia Sweet Onion. With a sharp knife, cut off the top of the onion. Make several criss cross cuts from top to bottom, cutting almost through the onion. Drop into ice water. If desired, tint water with food coloring of your choice. Chill several hours. When ready to serve, remove the onion from ice water and place on relish tray. Spread onion petals to form full bloom "flower". The petals are broken apart with the fingers and eaten with Creamy Olive Dip.

A Friend

VIDALIA SWEET ONION AND CHEESE DIP

1	8-ounce package cream cheese	1	teaspoon white vinegar
1	egg	1	stalk celery, finely chopped
1	pat butter (not margarine)	1	teaspoon white sugar
1	medium Vidalia Sweet Onion, chopped fine	½	teaspoon salt

Soften cream cheese in microwave or at room temperature in medium size bowl. Scramble egg in pat of butter and add to cream cheese. Add finely chopped onion and finely chopped celery, vinegar, sugar and salt. Mix all ingredients together. Chill for several hours in refrigerator or overnight. Mix well before serving with cut up veggies (celery pieces, pepper pieces, cucumbers, carrot sticks, cauliflower and broccoli pieces). Makes at least 20-24 dips or about 2 cups.

Carol S. Selak
York, PA

VIDALIA SWEET ONION WEDGIES

2	cups sliced Vidalia Sweet Onions		Salt and pepper to taste
2	tablespoons butter	1	egg
1	can refrigerated crescent rolls	¼	cup evaporated milk

Preheat oven to 400 degrees. Sauté onions in butter until golden brown and tender. Separate rolls into triangles. Place in ungreased round 8-inch pan, pressing together to form an even crust on bottom and halfway up the sides. Spread onions on top of dough. Season well with salt and pepper. Beat egg slightly; add evaporated milk. Pour over onions. Bake at 400 degrees for 20-25 minutes. Cut into wedges. Serve hot! Can be a perfect appetizer in small wedgies or as a vegetable with dinner.

Annetta Gajewski
Bridsboro, PA

VIDALIA SWEET ONION HORS D'OEUVRES

6	Vidalia Sweet Onions	½	cup cider vinegar
2	cups boiling water	1½	cups mayonnaise
1	cup sugar		

Cut onions into thin slices. Combine water, sugar and cider vinegar. Stir well until sugar is dissolved. Pour over onions. Cover and store overnight. Squeeze dry between paper towels. Place in bowl and mix with mayonnaise. Serve on saltines.

"Before mixing with mayonnaise, I take scissors and cut onions into small pieces."

Adrienne Lidbeck
Chatham, MA

Breads
&
Loaves

BLAND FARMS

BROCCOLI CORNBREAD

4 eggs, beaten
1 teaspoon salt
   Dash Louisiana hot
   pepper sauce
1 cup cottage cheese
1 stick margarine, melted
1 large Vidalia Sweet Onion,
      diced

1 10-ounce package frozen
      chopped broccoli, thawed
1 8½-ounce box corn muffin
      mix

Mix all ingredients. Put in a greased 9-inch pan or iron skillet and bake at 400 degrees for 30 to 40 minutes until golden brown. Enjoy! Yields 8 generous servings.
Variations: Substitute extra onion or lightly stir-fried chopped zucchini squash for the broccoli.

" So simple, yet so delicious for a special brunch for your company."

John B. Bienvenu
St. Martinville, LA

VIDALIA SWEET ONION RING LOAF

4 to 6 Vidalia Sweet Onions
1 cup milk
3 eggs, beaten
   Salt to taste

2 cups pancake mix
   Oil (for deep frying)
   Parsley

Slice onions and separate into rings. Soak rings in mixture of milk, eggs and salt in bowl for 30 minutes. Dip each onion ring in pancake mix and fry in oil heated to 375 degrees until golden brown. Pack fried onions loosely, not firmly, (without pressing) into an 8x4-inch loaf pan, and bake at 400 degrees for 10 to 15 minutes. Turn onto serving plate and garnish with parsley.
Serves 4.

"Great served with barbequed ribs, steak or hamburgers."

Elizabeth Partridge
Newport Beach, CA
Elva L. Valentine
Whittier, CA

VIDALIA SWEET ONION UPSIDE DOWN BREAD

2	or 3 medium sized Vidalia Sweet Onions	4	teaspoons baking powder
		1	teaspoon salt
3	tablespoons butter or margarine, divided	2	teaspoons white sugar
		1	egg, beaten
3	tablespoons brown sugar	1	cup milk
2	cups flour	¼	cup oil

Peel and thickly slice onions. Sauté onions in 2 tablespoons butter until golden and fairly soft. Spread remaining tablespoon butter in 9-inch round baking dish. Sprinkle evenly with brown sugar. Arrange onion slices in baking dish. For topping, combine flour, baking powder, salt and sugar. Beat egg, milk and oil; add to flour. Batter should be a little thinner than biscuit dough. Spread over top of onions. Bake 35 to 40 minutes in 350 degree oven. Let stand 5 minutes, loosen edges and turn out onto a plate. Cut in wedges to serve: Yield 6 servings.
Note: You may use 2 cups packaged baking mix in place of dry ingredients and proceed as directed above.

Ivah D. Stratton
Brockport, NY

THREE GRAIN FILLED
VIDALIA SWEET ONION RINGS

2	8 to 10-ounces each Vidalia sweet onions	1	teaspoon baking powder
		1	teaspoon baking soda
⅓	cup flour	½	cup buttermilk
3	tablespoons cornmeal	2	egg whites
3	tablespoons oat bran	2	tablespoons vegetable oil
2	teaspoons sugar		

Peel onions and cut crosswise into ½-inch slices. Remove centers of onion slices to leave ½-inch thick rings. Reserve centers and end pieces for other uses. Mix all ingredients together. Place onion rings on lightly oiled griddle, heated to 350 degrees. Fill each ring with batter. Cook until bottom sides begin to brown. Turn and cook until other side is done. Serve hot as appetizer or as an accompaniment to meat and vegetables. Serves 4 to 6.

Carrie Phelps
Hillsboro, NH

Salads

&

Salad Dressings

BEVERLY'S ORANGE~VIDALIA SWEET ONION SALAD

6	oranges, sliced or chunked	2	to 3 tablespoons honey
2	medium Vidalia Sweet Onions, sliced (may sauté in oil to soften)	½	clove garlic, crushed
		1	tablespoon celery seed
		1	tablespoon basil
6	tablespoons oil (olive is best, but any will do)	1	teaspoon oregano
3	tablespoons apple cider vinegar		

For dressing, mix oil, cider vinegar, honey, garlic, celery seed, basil and oregano together. Pour over oranges and onions and mix well. Chill. Serve on lettuce leaf. Yields 6 servings.

Note: Blueberries, raspberries or melons can also be eaten with Vidalias in a salad using the same dressing.

Beverly A. Mussari
Cincinnati, OH

CASUAL CALIFORNIA SALAD

1	small head cauliflower	⅓	cup sugar
3	large broccoli stalks	½	cup nuts: cashews, sunflower or pine nuts
1	medium Vidalia Sweet Onion, chopped	½	cup raisins
1	cup light mayonnaise	½	pound bacon, fried crisp and broken into pieces
1	cup sour cream		
4	tablespoons red wine vinegar		

Cut cauliflower and broccoli into bite-sized pieces and add Vidalia onion. Combine mayonnaise, sour cream, red wine vinegar and sugar together. Pour over vegetable mixture and mix well. Cover tightly and refrigerate 24 hours before serving. Just before serving, add nuts, raisins and bacon. Serves 16.

"This is wonderful served in the summer in place of vegetables with BBQ beef or chicken or with ham."

Janice McNees
Sun Valley, CA

COLORADO MACARONI SALAD

1	8-ounce package small shell macaroni	½	cup sharp Cheddar cheese
1	cup coarsely chopped celery	½	cup Monterey Jack cheese
1	cup coarsely chopped green pepper	½	cup soft processed cheese
1	cup coarsely chopped Vidalia Sweet Onions	⅔	cup mayonnaise (or to taste)

Cook macaroni as directed on package. Drain and rinse in cold water. Add chopped celery, green pepper and onion. Cut cheeses into small cubes and combine with other ingredients. Add mayonnaise, mixing well. Refrigerate until time to serve. Serves 10 to 12 people.
Note: This salad keeps well in the refrigerator for a week.

"Your onions are superb! Everything you say about them is true!"

Betsey L. Ford
Port Hueneme, CA

CORN, TOMATO AND VIDALIA SWEET ONION SALAD

1½	cups diced ripe tomatoes	⅛	teaspoon salt
⅓	cup chopped Vidalia Sweet Onion	1	tablespoon olive oil
2	medium ears fresh corn, cooked and cooled	15	fresh basil leaves
			Ground pepper
1	tablespoon plus 1 teaspoon balsamic vinegar		Salt

Combine tomatoes and onions. Scrape corn and juice off cobs. This should be about 1 cup. Add corn to tomatoes and onions. Whisk together vinegar and ⅛ teaspoon salt. Add oil and whisk. Stack basil leaves and slice into shreds. Add to tomato mixture. Combine vinegar mixture with vegetables and toss to coat. Season with pepper and salt. Cover and refrigerate 1 hour to 2 days. Serves 4.
Note: This salad is good with grilled fish.

Elizabeth Morrow
Woodland Hills, CA

CORNBREAD SALAD

1	small, 8-9 inch prepared cake of cornbread	1	cup diced sweet peppers, red or green
1	16-ounce can hot chili beans, drained	½	pound bacon, fried, crushed into bacon bits
1	cup Vidalia Sweet Onions, chopped	1¼	cup mayonnaise
1	cup diced tomatoes	¼	to ½ cup dill pickle juice
			Dill pickles, optional

Cool cornbread. Break up into small bits and place in an 9x13-inch oblong dish. On top of cornbread, make a layer of beans, then a layer of onions, then tomatoes, then sweet peppers and a layer of bacon. Mix mayonnaise and dill pickle juice together and spread on top layered salad. Take a fork and open up all the layers so the mayonnaise can go to the bottom. For a dressier salad, place slices of dill pickles on top. Serves 15.

Shirley S. Langston
Bessemer, AL

COUNTRY CLUB VIDALIA SWEET ONIONS

6	large Vidalia Sweet Onions, thinly sliced and separated into rings	½	cup vinegar
		1	tablespoon sugar
		1	teaspoon salt
2	cups water	½	cup mayonnaise
2	cups ice cubes	1	to 2 tablespoons celery seed

Soak onion rings 2 to 4 hours or overnight in water to which ice, vinegar, sugar and salt have been added. Cover container well and refrigerate. Drain well on paper towels; place in bowl. Combine mayonnaise and celery seed together and pour over onions. Toss to cover uniformly. Serves 20.

"This is ideal for picnics and cold suppers."

Gay S. Holsapple
Bartlesville, OK

CRUNCHY, COLD PEA SALAD

1   10-ounce package frozen green peas, thawed and not cooked

1   small Vidalia Sweet Onion, thinly sliced

¼   cup sunflower seeds

¼   cup Italian or French salad dressing

½   cup chopped celery, optional

Combine all ingredients and mix well. Peas should be *very cold* but not frozen inside. This is the secret to success of this salad - *all ingredients cold*. Serves 4.

Martha Gene Rank
Arlington, TX

DIABETIC, LO-CAL, DIETARY SNACK OR MEAL

3   ¼-inch slices Vidalia Sweet Onions

1   Italian or locally grown tomato

3   celery heart stalks

1   tablespoon mayonnaise or salad dressing, light

1½ tablespoons your favorite bottled cheese spread

Salt, light

Salt Vidalia Sweet Onion slices lightly. Remove white core from inside tomato stem end and cut tomatoes length wise and then cross wise 3 times. Lightly salt the 8 tomato pieces. Spread with mayonnaise. Wash celery stalks and cut off leaves. Cut stalks into 3 pieces, cross-wise. If only outer stalks are available, scrape off strings from outside of stalks. Salt stalks lightly with light salt. Have cheese spread at room temperature. Fill inside of stalk pieces with cheese spread. Arrange on luncheon plate with tomatoes and onions and enjoy!

Note: For complete meal, add one thin slice deli spiced roast beef or one cup cheese soup or a Vidalia Sweet Onion Sandwich.

"I am a Type II diabetic, addicted to Vidalia Sweet Onions for dietary reasons. Others may find my recipe similarly addictive!"

Dr. John J. Dougherty
Prescott, AZ

ENGLISH SUMMER SALAD

1	15-ounce can French cut beans, drained	2	Italian type tomatoes
1	15-ounce can black beans, drained	1	teaspoon chopped garlic
			Salt and pepper to taste
3	small new potatoes	1	large head of Boston lettuce
1	large Vidalia Sweet Onion	1	tablespoon olive oil
1	cup chopped celery	1	teaspoon safflower oil
		1	teaspoon lemon juice
		2	tablespoons malt vinegar

Rinse beans. Boil potatoes and slice. Cut onion, celery and tomatoes into small pieces. Finely chop garlic. Mix beans, potatoes, onions, celery, tomatoes and garlic. Add salt and pepper. Rinse and dry lettuce. Place around a large glass or china bowl (not wooden). Place vegetables in center of bowl. Stir together olive oil, safflower oil, lemon juice and malt vinegar and sprinkle on top of vegetables. Reserve some of the dressing and place in cup beside the salad so guests can add more if desired. Serves 6-8.

"I just LOVE Vidalia Sweet Onions and they make this salad taste so much better!"

Clive Harrison
New York City, NY

GERMAN POTATO SALAD

6	large potatoes, boiled with skins on		Salt and pepper
		½	teaspoon celery salt
1	Vidalia Sweet Onion		Tarragon vinegar, equal to
3	eggs, hard boiled		the amount of bacon
½	pound bacon, fried crisp, save drippings		drippings
		½	cup sugar

Cut up potatoes, onions and eggs into desired size. Sprinkle with salt, pepper and celery salt. In a small pan, bring bacon drippings to a boil. Add an equal amount of Tarragon vinegar, and ½ cup sugar. Boil about 1 minute. Pour over potato mix. Taste. Adjust seasonings if necessary. Crumble bacon and add to mixture. Serve warm.

A Friend

ITALIAN-PASTA-VIDALIA SWEET ONION SALAD

1   pound curly macaroni, cooked
1   8-ounce bottle Caesar or Italian salad dressing
3   hard cooked boiled eggs, sliced
1   cup black or green olives

2   cups Vidalia Sweet Onions, sliced and sautéed in oil for 3 to 5 minutes
1   tablespoon basil
1   tablespoon oregano
    Pepper to taste

Combine all ingredients and chill. Serves 5 to 6.

Note: If desired, diced, cooked chicken or ham can be added.

Beverly A. Mussari
Cincinnati, OH

ITALIAN SALAD

3   tomatoes, sliced crosswise into bite-sized crescent shaped pieces
½   Vidalia Sweet Onion, sliced in thin lengthwise strips

3   to 4 fresh basil leaves or ½ teaspoon crushed dry basil
3   tablespoons olive oil
    Salt & pepper to taste

Mix all ingredients and toss lightly. Allow to marinate for at least 1 hour. Serves 5.
Tip: Soak white bread in any excess juice.

"This recipe is straight from Italy, brought here by my husband's mother. It was a favorite in their family as it is in ours."

Marie Faraca
Spokane, WA

KIDNEY BEAN SALAD

2	cans red kidney beans	3	carrots, diced
4	sticks celery, finely chopped	½	green pepper, diced
1	Vidalia Sweet Onion, finely chopped	1	clove garlic, finely chopped
			Salt
4	tablespoons sweet pickles, finely diced		Pepper
			Light mayonnaise, enough to moisten
3	hard cooked eggs, chopped		Lettuce, for serving

Rinse and drain kidney beans well. Add finely chopped ingredients, salt and pepper, then just enough mayonnaise to moisten. Chill. Serve on a bed of lettuce with more sliced Vidalia Sweet Onions. Serves 4.

Gail Diane Hardwick
Houston, TX

POTATO SALAD

2	pounds medium potatoes	¾	cup chopped celery
1	cup Vidalia Sweet Onion, chopped	⅛	teaspoon pepper
1	teaspoon salt	1	tablespoon finely diced parsley (optional)
¼	cup Italian dressing	½	cup mayonnaise
4	eggs, cooked and chopped		

Cook potatoes with skins in salted water until done. Cool, peel and slice into bowl. Add Vidalia Sweet Onion, salt and Italian dressing. Mix well. Cover and marinate in refrigerator for 2 or 3 hours. Before serving, stir in eggs, chopped celery, pepper, parsley and mayonnaise. Serves 8.
Note: Flavor is best if potatoes are warm when combined with onion and Italian dressing.

Jean Wyrill
Kirivin, KS

MY HUSBANDS FAVORITE CARROT SALAD

1   cup firmly grated Vidalia
     Sweet Onion
3   cups grated carrots

¾   cup salad dressing

Mix all ingredients and blend well. Store in refrigerator. Serves 8.

Virginia Strating
Fulton, IL

MARINATED VIDALIA SWEET ONION AND MIXED VEGETABLE SALAD

1   14-ounce can artichoke
     hearts, quartered, drained
1   14-ounce can hearts of palm,
     sliced (optional), drained
1   14-ounce can pitted ripe
     olives, small, drained
1   2-ounce jar diced pimentos or
     ½ cup diced red pepper,
     drained
2   medium Vidalia Sweet Onions,
     cut into slivers
8   ounces fresh mushrooms,
     sliced

DRESSING:
1   clove garlic, pressed
1   teaspoon salt
¼   teaspoon pepper
¼   cup minced fresh parsley
½   teaspoon dried thyme
⅔   cup vegetable oil
¼   cup red wine vinegar
1   tablespoon sugar

Combine artichoke hearts, hearts of palm, olives, pimentos and onions (or red pepper). Combine dressing ingredients and pour over vegetables. Marinate overnight. Add mushrooms just before serving. May serve in bowl lined with leaf type lettuce. Yields 6 servings.

Rebecca Larson
Viroqua, WI

RON'S SIMPLE AND DELICIOUS PEPPERS

Peppers of your choice
Vidalia Sweet Onion, coarsely
    chopped

American or Cheddar smoky
    flavored cheese, shredded
Salt to taste

Depending on type and size of pepper, either cut in half lengthwise or make a lengthwise cut on one side. Cut out stem, veins and seeds. Lay pepper on side. Fill approximately ½ full with Vidalia Sweet Onion, then cheese. Close like a taco and enjoy. Yields ½ to 1 pepper per serving.

Ronald F. LaMar
Bettendorf, IA

SAUTÉED ONIONS/HEARTS OF CELERY WITH A TWIST

3   Vidalia Sweet Onions, sliced
2   cups celery hearts, sliced
¼   cup butter
2   cups chicken broth

⅓   cup lemon juice
4   slivers lemon rind
Salt
Pepper

Sauté onions and celery in butter until soft. Marinate in broth, lemon juice, salt, pepper and lemon rind. When cool, refrigerate.

Note: Serve as an accompaniment with roast, chicken, or fish entrees.

Marilyn Geraty
Sacramento, CA

SCANDINAVIAN SALAD

1   can peas, green (or sweet)   MARINADE:
1   can French style green beans   Scant cup sugar
1   4-ounce jar chopped pimento   ½   cup corn oil
1   Vidalia Sweet Onion, chopped   ½   cup vinegar
        or thinly sliced

Drain peas, beans and pimento. Mix with Vidalia Sweet Onion. Cover with marinade and let stand overnight. Serves 8.

"This can be used as a vegetable. Keeps a long time in the refrigerator."

Mrs. Arthur Nuttall, Jr.
Seneca, SC

SOME KINDA SALAD

1   large Vidalia sweet onion,   DRESSING:
        sliced thinly   ½   cup olive oil
1   large ripe tomato, sectioned   ½   red wine vinegar
1   avocado, sliced   1   teaspoon Dijon mustard
     Bleu cheese

Divide onion, tomato, and avocado into 2 bowls or salad plates. Combine ingredients for dressing and shake thoroughly. Pour over vegetables and refrigerate for at least 1 hour. Crumble Bleu cheese on top before serving.

Barbara Phinney
Sandpoint, ID

ORANGE AND ONION SALAD

Vidalia Sweet Onions
Navel oranges

French dressing

On individual salad plates, alternate slices of Vidalia Sweet Onions with slices of navel oranges. Top with creamy French dressing.

"Dee-lish-ous!"

Bob and Gloria Halliday
Potsdam, NY

TOMATO SALAD

1   medium ripe tomato
1   to 2 medium Vidalia Sweet
      Onions
1   to 2 hot peppers or ½ green
      bell pepper

Salt and Pepper, to taste
Oregano
Basil
Olive oil

Cut tomatoes, onions, and peppers into bite-sized pieces. Put in a large salad bowl; add salt and pepper. Sprinkle with oregano and basil. Toss with olive oil.

"Must be served with fresh Italian bread to sop up tomato juice and oil mixture when salad is gone."

Mrs. Arthur A. Yann, Jr.
Pittsburgh, PA

TOMATO AND ONION SALAD

4	firm tomatoes	French dressing
1	medium Vidalia Sweet Onion	

Cut tomatoes into ¼-inch slices. Thinly slice onion and place alternately in salad bowl with tomatoes. Cover with French or tomato soup dressing. Serves 4 to 5.

"This makes a delicious, refreshing salad for summertime."

Mrs. James Shuping
Phoenix, AZ

TUNA SALAD

1	6½-ounce can tuna (white albacore packed in water)	½	cup finely chopped pecans (optional)
2	hard cooked eggs, diced	2½	tablespoons light mayonnaise
1	Vidalia Sweet Onion, peeled and finely diced		Salt
			Pepper

Combine all ingredients. Serve chilled.
Serving suggestions: Serve on whole-wheat bread; stuffed in tomatoes; on bed of lettuce or serve alone or on cracker of your choice.

Gail Diane Hardwick
Houston, TX

VIDALIA ONIONS WITH BALSAMIC VINEGAR

4	Vidalia Sweet Onions	Salt
5	tablespoons balsamic vinegar	Pepper, freshly ground
¼	cup (approximately) extra virgin olive oil	

Peel the onions leaving root intact. Cut each onion into 8 wedges. Place the onion wedges in a marinating container (glass or plastic). Drizzle vinegar over onion wedges. Close the container and marinate 20 to 30 minutes, turning to distribute the vinegar occasionally. Preheat broiler. Cover a baking sheet with foil. Drain the onions and reserve the vinegar. Arrange the onions in a single layer on the baking sheet. Brush lightly with oil on all sides and sprinkle with salt and pepper. Broil until browned but not charred; turn over and broil other side until browned but not charred. Transfer to serving dish and sprinkle with 1½ tablespoons of the reserved vinegar. May be served hot or at room temperature. If served at room temperature, this can be prepared 8 hours ahead. Serves 4.

Susan C. Burgess
Georgetown, DE

VIDALIA-BEEF VINAIGRETTE

4	Vidalia Sweet Onions	4	tablespoons olive oil
½	to ¾ pound cold roast beef		Salt to taste
1	to 2 tablespoons vinegar		Pepper to taste

Peel onions and slice very thin. Cut beef into ½-inch cubes. Toss onions and beef gently. Combine vinegar, oil, salt and pepper. Pour on dressing and toss again. Refrigerate ½ hour to allow flavors to blend.
Serves 3 to 4.
Serving suggestions: Serve with crunchy bread and a good red wine.

" If onions are exceptionally large, increase the amount of dressing. Absolutely essential to use Vidalia sweet onions for this recipe. No others will do!"

June Sutton
Watertown, CT

VIDALIA COLESLAW WITH CAPERS

1	small head cabbage	3	tablespoons olive oil
1	medium Vidalia Sweet Onion	½	teaspoon Tabasco sauce
	Salt	1	teaspoon fresh parsley
	Pepper	2	tablespoon capers
2	tablespoons wine vinegar	1	cup mayonnaise

Shred cabbage and finely chop onion. Add remaining ingredients and toss. Chill. Makes about 4 cups.

"This recipe is great with fried catfish."

Holly Wagner
Wheaton, IL

VIDALIA ONION AND CUCUMBER TOSS

2	Vidalia Sweet Onions, sliced		Pepper to taste
3	cucumbers sliced	2	tablespoons water
1	tablespoon sugar	4	tablespoons wine vinegar
1	teaspoon salt		

Slice onions into ¼-inch slices and separate into rings if desired. Peel cucumbers and score with tines of fork. Slice into ⅛-inch slices. Put onions and cucumbers in a bowl and sprinkle with sugar, salt and pepper. Add water and vinegar. Toss lightly. Let stand 15 to 20 minutes before serving to mingle flavors. Serves 4 to 6.

Virginia F. Campbell
Selden, NY

VIDALIA ONION SALAD

1	cup cider vinegar	1	teaspoon chopped parsley
½	cup water	½	teaspoon basil
¾	cup sugar	3	large Vidalia Sweet Onions,
	Dash cayenne		sliced
1	teaspoon salt		Cucumber slices, optional

Combine vinegar, water, sugar, cayenne, salt, parsley and basil together in jar. Shake until sugar is dissolved. Pour over onions and chill. Cucumber slices can be added. Will keep in refrigerator almost forever if covered. Serve on lettuce leaf or in bowl. Serves 6 to 8.

"Dressing is great for tossed salad after onions are gone."

James L. Brown
Indianapolis, IN

VIDALIA SWEET ONION SALAD SUPREME

1	jumbo Vidalia Sweet Onion,	½	pound Genoa salami, sliced
	sliced very thin		thin
2	large ripe tomatoes, sliced		Italian salad dressing
	about ¼-inch		

In a square dish (sides must be at least 2 inches deep) arrange sliced onions, tomatoes and salami alternately in rows so they do not lie down flat. Pour just enough Italian dressing over the salad to moisten all ingredients. For best taste, cover and marinate in refrigerator until cold. Spoon salad dressing from bottom of dish over ingredients before serving. Serves 4.

Note: This is a quick and delicious dish and can be served as a salad or an appetizer. Good for pot-luck meals, picnics, and cook-outs as well as a nice presentation at formal dinners.

Alternates: This dish is also delicious with substitution of pepperoni for salami; or without any meat at all - just the onions, tomatoes, and salad dressing.

Phil Bergelt
St. Cloud, FL

VIDALIA ONIONS AND TOMATOES

1	Vidalia Sweet Onion, sliced into ¼-inch slices		**DRESSING:**
2	tomatoes, sliced into ¼-inch slices	1	tablespoon balsamic vinegar
		3	tablespoons olive oil
		1	teaspoon mustard powder

Place onion and tomato slices on a plate. Mix vinegar, oil and mustard powder; stir well. Pour on top of onions and tomatoes. Serves 2.
Note: Your favorite salad dressing can be used in place of dressing listed above.

"Very good indeed."

Jonathan Bloomberg
New York, NY

VIDALIA ONION AND TOMATO SALAD

2	Vidalia sweet onions	2	tablespoons olive oil
2	ripe tomatoes	2	balsamic vinegar
	Fresh basil		

Cut onions and tomatoes into very thin slices about ¼ to ⅛-inch thick. Place in a bowl. Chop basil into shreds and add to onions and tomatoes. Stir in olive oil and vinegar.
Note: The portions of olive oil and vinegar may vary with different brands. Taste dressing as you go along and adjust according to your taste.

"We wait all year for these onions and the wait is worth it!"

Frances Nordenschild
Cranbury, NJ

VIDALIA REVELRY

2	Vidalia Sweet Onions	Vinegar and oil dressing	
2	to 3 medium fresh tomatoes	Italian dressing mix	
1	medium cucumber		

Slice onions, tomatoes and cucumber to desired thickness. (Mix vinegar and oil dressing according to bottle directions. Pour in ½ package dried Italian dressing mix.) Combine onions, tomatoes, and cucumbers. Pour salad dressing (amount you would like) over the vegetables and mix well. Yields 3 to 4 cups.

Note: Good with hams or with any favorite lunch or dinner.

Mrs. J. H. Hankins
Bartlesville, OK

VIDALIA SWEET ONION SALAD

4	large Vidalia Sweet Onions, sliced in rings	2	tablespoons sugar
1	teaspoon vinegar	½	teaspoon salt
2	tablespoons mayonnaise	½	teaspoon pepper

Put onions in colander. Pour boiling water over onions, then plunge onions into a bowl of ice water. Drain. Blend remaining ingredients together and add onions. Mix well. Serves 6.

Note: Very good with fish.

Margaret Bieda
Oconto Falls, WI

VINE LA VIDALIA SALADE

4   large Vidalia Sweet Onions, peeled and chopped
1   teaspoon tarragon wine vinegar
2   tablespoons mayonnaise, homemade preferred

2   tablespoons sugar, optional
½   teaspoon salt
½   teaspoon pepper
    Dried tarragon
    Lettuce for serving

Put onions in a colander and pour boiling water over them. Plunge onions into a bowl of iced water for a few minutes, then drain thoroughly. In mixing bowl, blend remaining ingredients. Add onions, pinch of dried tarragon and toss well. Serve well chilled in lettuce cup. Serves 4.

Shirley Holland
Wallingford, PA

WHITE BEAN, CAPER AND ONION SALAD

¼   cup olive oil
1   garlic clove, mashed
⅛   to ¼ teaspoon cayenne pepper
2   tablespoons vinegar

1   bottle capers, drained and well rinsed
1   Vidalia Sweet Onion, chopped coarsely
1   can white beans, drained (use cannelini or small white beans)

Mix olive oil with mashed garlic and cayenne. Stir in vinegar. Add capers, onions, and beans and toss gently to coat with vinaigrette. Take care not to mash beans. Serves 4.

"This is a quick and easy recipe. It's great to have as a side dish on hot summer nights, along with a pasta salad and fresh fruit."

Juanita Ackerman
Golden Bridge, NY

DELUXE THOUSAND ISLAND DRESSING

1 cup mayonnaise
2 tablespoons chili sauce
1 tablespoon dairy sour cream
½ teaspoon Dijon-type mustard

½ teaspoon fresh lemon juice
¼ cup chopped Vidalia Sweet Onion

Combine all ingredients and mix well. Refrigerate. Yields 1½ cups.

Jay M. Tischenkel
Beech Mountain, NC
Past President
Florida Restaurant Association

MUSTARD ONION DRESSING

⅓ cup vegetable oil
⅓ cup wine vinegar with garlic
⅔ cup sugar
3 tablespoons prepared mustard

1 cup chopped Vidalia Sweet Onion
1 teaspoon salt

Put all ingredients into blender or small food processor and mix until well blended. Yields 1 pint.
Note: May be stored in refrigerator for several weeks. Delicious with fresh spinach, mushrooms, or fresh Vidalia Onion Ring Salad. Can be used as a dip for vegetables. Also good dressing for shredded cabbage.

Vera Flanigan
Camp Hill, PA

VIDALIA SWEET ONION SALAD DRESSING

1 cup sugar	1 Vidalia Sweet Onion, grated
1 teaspoon salt	½ to ¾ cup vinegar
1 teaspoon dry mustard	1 to 2 tablespoons oil
1 teaspoon celery seed	

In a small saucepan, mix first 4 ingredients. Add grated Vidalia Sweet Onion (size depends on individual taste), oil and vinegar. Heat until sugar is melted. Cool and refrigerate. Yields 1½ to 2 cups.
Note: Reheat and use to wilt lettuce or serve cold on any vegetables. Keeps in refrigerator indefinitely.

Mary T. Baker
Jacksonville, AL

VIDALIA VINEGAR

8 ounces white vinegar	½ cup quartered and sliced
Several sprigs of fresh	Vidalia Sweet Onions
rosemary	2 tablespoons honey
½ cup raisins	
¼ cup orange peel, slivered	

Place all ingredients in a bottle with a plastic or glass lid. Let stand several days in cool place. Ready to use on fruits or salads.

Beverly A. Mussari
Cincinnati, OH

Soups
&
Sandwiches

BEST ONION SOUP

10	large Vidalia Sweet Onions, sliced, divided	2	cups water
1	cup butter, divided	3	teaspoons browning and seasoning sauce
2	10½-ounce cans beef bouillon		Salt
3	10½-ounce cans consommé		Pepper
1½	cups dry white wine	¼	cup cognac
			Parmesan cheese

Sauté ½ the onions in ½ the butter. Cook gently. Repeat with remainder of onions and butter. Place in soup kettle. Add liquids. Bring to boil and simmer for 30 minutes. Season. Add cognac before eating and reheat. Sprinkle with Parmesan. Can be cooked a day ahead or frozen.

Yields 5 to 6 pints.

Note: ½ cup butter may be substituted for 1 cup if desired.

Mrs. A.C. Brown, Jr.
North Kingstown, RI

CORN CHOWDER

5	medium potatoes, peeled and diced	1	15-ounce can creamed style corn with liquid
1	small Vidalia Sweet Onion, diced into large pieces	1½	to 2 cups milk
	Salt, to taste		Salt
			Pepper
1	17-ounce can whole kernel corn with liquid	½	stick butter

Cover potatoes and onions with water; add salt. Cook until tender, about 15 minutes. Drain and add whole kernel and creamed style corn, then milk to proper consistency. Add more salt if needed and pepper. Heat on low, stirring occasionally until piping hot. Add butter and let melt. Serves 4 to 6.

Note: Serve with crusty French bread.

"Great on a cold winter night!"

Joyce McDonald
Upper Marlboro, MD

COLD CREAM OF VIDALIA ONION SOUP

5	slices of lean bacon, cut crosswise into ½-inch strips	1	bay leaf
½	cup (1 stick) unsalted butter	1	cup heavy cream, well chilled
3	pounds (about 10) Vidalia Sweet Onions, sliced thin	1	cup crème fraîche
8	garlic cloves	3	tablespoons fresh lemon juice
4	cups chicken broth	⅛	teaspoon Tabasco
2	cups dry white wine	⅛	teaspoon freshly grated nutmeg
1	tablespoon fresh thyme or 1 teaspoon crumbled dried thyme		Salt and pepper, to taste
		2	cups croutons
		1	cup thinly sliced scallion

In a heavy kettle, cook the bacon over moderate heat, stirring occasionally until crisp. Using a slotted spoon, transfer bacon to paper towels. Drain off bacon grease and reserve. Add the butter to the kettle. Then add onions and garlic and cook covered over low heat, stirring occasionally, for 25 to 30 minutes or until onions and garlic are colored lightly and softened. Add chicken broth, wine, thyme, and bay leaf; cover and simmer for 20 minutes. Discard bay leaf. In a blender or food processor, puree the mixture in batches. Strain into a bowl, pressing hard on the solids. Cover and chill for 3 to 4 hours or until it is cold. Whisk in the heavy cream, the crème fraîche, lemon juice, Tabasco, and nutmeg. Season with salt and pepper. Serve the soup in chilled bowls sprinkled with croutons, scallion, and reserved bacon. Serves 8.

Crème fraîche: Stir one teaspoon of buttermilk into one cup of heavy cream. Heat mixture gently to a lukewarm temperature (being careful not to overheat) over low heat. Remove from heat and allow to stand at room temperature until mixture thickens. Chill and enjoy!

Courtesy of
The Fearrington House
Chapel Hill, NC
Submitted by
Donald S. Elrod
Pebble Beach, CA

CREAM OF ONION, POTATO, CHEESE SOUP

4	medium sized Vidalia Sweet Onions, finely chopped	8	cups homemade chicken broth (may use bouillon cubes)
7	medium sized mushrooms, sliced	1	envelope white sauce mix
2	tablespoons butter	8	ounces Velveeta mild Mexican cheese, cubed
6	medium sized red potatoes, finely chopped		
1	teaspoon seasoning blend or salt and pepper to taste		

Sauté onions and mushrooms in butter until limp. Add potatoes and seasonings; then add chicken broth and cook 20 to 30 minutes. Make white sauce following instructions on package and stir in cubed cheese. Add cheese sauce to soup mixture. Blend well. Serves 8 to 10.

Ernestine J. Shutt
San Jose, CA

CREAM OF SWEET ONION AND SAUTERNE SOUP

½	cup (1 stick) unsalted butter	4	cups sauterne wine
4	Vidalia sweet onions, sliced lengthwise into thin slivers	2	quarts chicken stock
3	tablespoons sugar	2½	cups whipping cream
¼	cup unbleached all purpose flour		Salt
			Freshly ground pepper, to taste
			Snipped chives for garnish

In stockpot over medium-high heat, melt butter. Stir in onions and cook stirring constantly 5 minutes. Reduce heat to low. Place sheet of waxed paper on top of onions and leave about 20 minutes, or until onions are very tender and translucent. Remove and discard waxed paper. Stir in sugar and cook onions 3 minutes to caramelize. Stir in flour and cook another 2 minutes. Gradually whisk in wine and chicken stock. Simmer soup uncovered 10 minutes. Stir cream into soup and season to taste with salt and pepper. Keep soup warm over low heat until ready to serve. Garnish with a few chives in center of each serving. Serves 8 to 10.

Janet Karmirski
Milwaukee, WI

CREAM OF VIDALIA ONION SOUP

1	pound Vidalia Sweet Onions	1½	teaspoons sherry
1	parsnip		Salt
2	stalks celery		Freshly ground pepper to taste
5	strips bacon, chopped	½	cup whipping cream
1	clove garlic, minced		Cayenne pepper
½	cup apple cider		Salt and pepper, to taste
2¾	cup chicken stock	2	tablespoons fresh chives
	Bouquet garni (bay leaf,		Nutmeg
	thyme, and parsley, tied		
	in a cheesecloth bundle)		

In food processor, finely chop onions, parsnip and celery. In large saucepan, cook bacon over medium heat for 5 to 6 minutes or until pieces are crisp. With slotted spoon, transfer bacon to a plate lined with paper towel. Reserve 2 tablespoons fat in pan. Add onions, parsnip, celery and garlic and cook 4 minutes or until vegetables are soft but not brown. Add cider, stock, bouquet garni, sherry and salt and pepper. Bring soup to a boil. Reduce heat and simmer 20 minutes or until vegetables are very soft. Remove bouquet garni. Purée soup in the food processor and return to pan. Just before serving, stir in cream and heat to simmer. Season with cayenne pepper and nutmeg, to taste. Add salt and pepper. Sprinkle soup with reserved bacon and chives. Serves 4.

"As an onion lover, Vidalia onions are an extra-special treat for me! One of my favorite ways of eating them is whole, grilled in foil with a little butter, salt and pepper."

Lorraine Entrikin
North Wales, PA

FORK AND KNIFE ONION SOUP

3	medium Vidalia sweet onions		Salt
¼	cup margarine		Pepper
1	teaspoon all purpose flour	9	slices French bread, cut into
4	cups beef broth		½-inch slices
1	teaspoon Worcestershire sauce	2	cups grated Swiss cheese

Sauté thin slices of onion in margarine until lightly browned. Stir in flour. Gradually add broth, Worcestershire, salt and pepper and simmer 10 minutes. Layer half the bread and cheese in a 3-quart casserole, add soup, top with rest of bread. Sprinkle with remaining cheese. Place in oven and bake at 400 degrees for 15 minutes or until golden brown. Serves 4 to 6.

"Served with salad it's a meal"

Martha Taylor
Maumee, OH

FRENCH ONION SOUP I

1	large or 2 medium Vidalia sweet onions	1	slice bread
			Parmesan or Romano grated
1	stick margarine or butter		cheese
1	10¾-ounce can consommé or bouillon	2	slices Mozzarella or Gruyére cheese

Butter both sides of bread and sprinkle top side heavily with Parmesan or Romano cheese. Toast and cut into 4 pieces. Set aside. Slice onions into thin rings and separate by cutting through once or tear into rings. Melt ½ stick margarine or butter in a large skillet. When foaming, add ½ the onions. Sauté until golden. In small saucepan, put consommé on warm and add cooked onions. Repeat procedure with remainder of margarine and onions. In bottom of crocks or ovenproof dishes, place a piece of the quartered toast and add soup. Top with another piece of quartered toast. Cover with cheese slices. Bake at 350 degrees for 10 minutes. May be placed under broiler until cheese is lightly brown. Serves 2.

Jane Bone
Cape Coral, FL

FRENCH ONION SOUP II
(THE VERY BEST)

4	slices French bread	3	10¾-ounce cans beef bouillon
3	tablespoons butter		
3	large Vidalia Sweet Onions, finely sliced	1	can beef broth
		4	tablespoons Parmesan cheese
1	tablespoon flour	4	slices Swiss or Mozzarella cheese
1	teaspoon freshly ground pepper		

Toast French bread slices. In a large saucepan, melt butter and sauté onions until clear in color. Add flour and stir constantly for 3 minutes. Stir in pepper; add beef bouillon and beef broth. Bring to a boil, lower heat and simmer for 30 minutes (covered with lid slightly tilted). When ready to serve, warm soup bowls slightly. Spoon soup into individual bowls and float one piece of toasted French bread in each. Sprinkle with Parmesan cheese. Cover each bowl completely with Swiss or Mozzarella cheese. Place bowls under broiler until cheese is slightly browned and bubbly. Serve immediately. Serves 4.

Jim Evered
Denton, TX

FRENCH ONION SOUP III

3	cups thinly sliced Vidalia sweet onions	2	tablespoons all purpose flour
¼	cup butter	1	quart beef bouillon or beef broth
1½	teaspoons salt		
½	cup sugar (aids browning)	1	cup grated Parmesan cheese

Slice Vidalia sweet onions. Brown slightly in melted butter. Cover and let cook for about 15 minutes. *Do not rush this part.* Uncover, add salt, sugar, and flour; stir well. Gradually add broth. If crock pot is used, cook covered on LOW 6 to 8 hours or on HIGH for 3 hours.

Robert P. Martin
Indiana, PA

ITALIAN ONION AND BREAD SOUP

5	to 6 tablespoons olive oil	6	cups dry white wine
8	large Vidalia Sweet Onions (approximately 6 pounds), halved and thinly sliced	1	cinnamon stick
		6	slices day old crusty bread, broken
1	tablespoon sugar		Salt
6	cups chicken broth		Parmigiano cheese, grated

Preheat oven to 350 degrees. Heat the oil in a large ovenproof saucepan or casserole over medium heat. Stir in onions and cook until pale yellow. Sprinkle with sugar and mix. Stir in the broth and wine. Add cinnamon stick and bring to a boil. Cover with a sheet of aluminum foil and place in oven. Cook 1 hour. Then add the bread and stir until smooth and thick. Cook uncovered 30 minutes. Discard cinnamon. Season with salt and sprinkle with Parmigiano.

Julia L. VanHees
Long Beach, CA

ONION SOUP AU GRATIN

6	large Vidalia Sweet Onions, sliced	½	teaspoon black pepper
2	tablespoons butter or margarine	6	slices toasted Italian or French bread
12	cups water	6	slices Swiss cheese
8	beef bouillon cubes	8	ounces shredded Mozzarella cheese
½	teaspoon crushed rosemary, dried	½	cup Parmesan cheese
1	teaspoon thyme		

Melt butter in large soup pot. Add onions and cook until golden brown. Add water, bouillon, and spices. Cook on low heat for 1 hour. Divide soup into 6 onion soup crocks or heat proof soup bowls. Place toasted bread on soup. Top each with 1 slice of Swiss cheese. Sprinkle with Mozzarella and Parmesan cheeses. Broil until cheeses melt and are golden brown. Serves 6.

"A family favorite for lunch or light dinner served with a salad"
Marylee Pratnicki
Long Branch, NJ

ONION & RED PEPPER SOUP

2	Vidalia Sweet Onions	2	dashes Tabasco or other hot sauce
2	tablespoons canola oil		
3	large red bell peppers	½	cup milk
1	cup chicken stock	1	cup cream
½	teaspoon salt		Sour cream, for serving
¼	teaspoon fresh ground white pepper		

Peel and slice the onions. Sauté in oil until limp, but do not allow to color. Remove the stems, seeds and membranes from the peppers and cut into chunks. Add the peppers to the onions and sauté for 1 minute. Add chicken stock, salt, pepper and hot sauce. Simmer until the vegetables are well cooked. Remove peppers and onions to a food processor or blender and purée. With the motor running, pour in the cooking liquid. Strain the mixture through a fine sieve to remove any pepper skin that has not been puréed. Add milk and cream and combine well. Serve hot or cold. Float a spoon of sour cream on top of each serving. Serves 6.

Betty King
Washington, DC

MONIQUE'S FRENCH ONION SOUP

4	to 6 large Vidalia Sweet Onions	½	teaspoon thyme
			Salt
6	tablespoons shortening		Pepper
1	can beef bouillon or ½ bottle Bovril	3	slices Mozzarella cheese
		6	slices crusty bread
6	cups water		

Slice onions. Simmer in shortening 10 minutes in large pot. Add beef bouillon or Bovril. Add water, thyme, salt and pepper. Simmer 1½ to 2 hours. Pour or ladle into small soup bowls with slice of crusty bread on bottom. Top with ½ slice Mozzarella cheese and microwave 30 to 40 seconds. Serves 6.

Barbara C. Phillips
Falls Church, VA

VIDALIA ONION RIVEL* SOUP

¼	cup butter or margarine	1	egg
2	cups sliced Vidalia sweet onions	¾	to 1 cup all purpose flour
		½	teaspoon salt
6	cups beef broth		Pepper, liberal amount

In a large saucepan, melt butter. Add onions and sauté over low heat until the onions are golden brown (about 7 to 8 minutes). Add broth and bring to a boil over medium heat. In the meantime, prepare the rivels. In a medium bowl, beat the eggs well. Add flour, salt and pepper. Mix first with a spoon and then finish mixing by rubbing the dough between your fingers. The largest pieces should be pea size. Sprinkle rivels slowly over boiling broth, stirring constantly but gently. Reduce heat to medium, cover; simmer about 8 to 10 minutes. Serve immediately.

Mrs. John Jody Tindall
Frankfort, IN

* *A "rivel" is a homemade noodle.*

VIDALIA SWEET ONION & MUSHROOM SOUP

¼	cup butter or margarine	½	cup water plus 2 tablespoons white wine
1½	cups Vidalia sweet onions, thinly sliced	2	teaspoons Worcestershire sauce
12	ounces fresh mushrooms, sliced	¼	teaspoon ground black pepper
5	packets powdered beef broth		
4	cups boiling water		

In a large saucepan, melt butter. Add onions and sauté for 15 minutes or until very soft. Add mushrooms and sauté 5 minutes. Stir in all other ingredients. Bring to a fast boil and reduce heat immediately to simmer. Cover and simmer for 15 minutes. Serves 4 as a main course or 6 as an appetizer.

Joan M. Ballard
Pacheco, CA

VIDALIA ONION SOUP

12	strips bacon	2	soup cans water
	Garlic clove	1	tablespoon Jalapeño mustard
4	shallots	2	bay leaves
¼	pound butter	2	ounces brandy, optional
2	tablespoons olive oil		Rosemary, pinch to taste
2	tablespoons water		Salt
8	Baby Vidalia Sweet Onions or		Pepper
	3 to 4 large Vidalia onions		Parmesan cheese
2	cans bouillon soup (approx.		Romano cheese
	10 oz)		Croutons

Cook bacon in large pot with garlic clove and shallots. Drain grease and retain bacon, garlic and shallots. Add butter to empty pot bacon was cooked in. Add olive oil and 2 tablespoons water to pot. Add onions and fry until brown. Add bouillon soup and 2 cans water. Stir in mustard, bay leaves, brandy, and rosemary. Add retained bacon, shallots and garlic. Bring to a boil; reduce heat and simmer covered for 2 hours. Season to taste with salt and pepper. Serve in crock. Cover top of soup with Parmesan and Romano cheese and croutons. Bake if desired.
Serves 6 to 8.

"May use Dijon mustard, but the Jalapeno from Bland Farms adds a little zest"

Stephen Polin
Yardley, PA

"BABYWICHES"

8	slices white and/or rye bread	2	tomatoes, sliced
4	Baby Vidalia Sweet Onions	¼	pound thinly sliced roast
	thinly sliced		beef, rare
¼	pound butter, softened		

Generously butter bread and layer roast beef, tomato and thinly sliced Baby Vidalias. Season with salt and pepper. Yields 4 closed sandwiches, cut into quarters.

"These sandwiches are Things Dreams are Made Of"

Pad McQuade
Valley Stream, NY

BASIL, ONION AND TOMATO SANDWICH (BOT)

1	Hero sandwich roll (also called Submarine, Grinder or Italian roll)	2	fully ripe plum tomatoes
		2	center slices Vidalia Sweet Onions, sliced ¼-inch thick
2	teaspoons olive oil	4	fresh basil leaves

Split the roll in half lengthwise and sprinkle each cut surface with olive oil. Slice the tomatoes lengthwise ¼-inch thick and place on the bottom half of the roll using the center slices. Cut the Vidalia sweet onion slices in half and place on top of the tomatoes. Coarsely chop basil leaves and sprinkle on top of the onion. Cover with the other half of the roll. Serves 1 hungry person or 2 dainty eaters.

"For calorie and fat conscious gourmets, try the BOT sandwich. A taste treat with succulent Vidalia sweet onions."

Francis Federighi
Schenectady, NY

GRILLED VIDALIA-PINEAPPLE SANDWICH

1	slice bread	1	slice pineapple
1	or 2 slices Vidalia Sweet Onion	1	slice ham or chicken
		1	slice Mozzarella cheese

Layer items on bread and top with cheese. Place under broiler until cheese melts. A great opened face sandwich.

"Use as an appetizer by making several and cutting into fourths."

Beverly A. Mussari
Cincinnati, OH

HOT DOGS AND ONIONS

Pat of butter or margarine
2   Vidalia Sweet Onions, jumbo

1   package hot dogs, cut in slices

Melt butter in large fry pan. Cut up onions and sauté in butter 10 minutes or less. Add cut up hot dogs and mix. Cover and heat until hot. Serve on hot dog buns or bread. Serves 4.

Patricia Kiertscher
Downers Grove, IL

OLD FASHIONED ONION SANDWICH

2   slices of your favorite bread
Butter
Vidalia Sweet Onion, sliced thin

Tomato, sliced and peeled
Salt
Pepper

Butter bread. Place thinly sliced Vidalia Sweet Onion slices on bread. Add tomato and salt and pepper to taste.

"Fried or scrambled egg may be substituted for tomato. Just a plain Vidalia sweet onion and bread with butter is perfect with a little salt and pepper to taste."

Lucille Anderson
Newbury Park, CA

ORANGE/ONION SANDWICH

Vidalia Sweet Onions
Orange slices
Bread of choice

Butter
Mayonnaise, if desired

Slice onions. Peel and slice oranges. Butter bread and layer with onion and orange slices. Top with mayonnaise if desired.

James A. Feicht
Kittanning, PA

ONION POCKET SANDWICH

2   tablespoons olive oil
1   Vidalia Sweet Onion
1   whole-wheat pocket bread

2   to 3 tablespoons of your
      favorite cheese, grated

Heat oil slightly in pan while slicing onion. Add onion, cook until clear. Fill pocket with cooked onion and cheese. Place under broiler and brown bread to your taste. Cheese will melt.
Note: Mushrooms may be added.

Mrs. Joseph Golas
Enfield, CT

OPEN~FACED VIDALIA SWEET ONION PEANUT BUTTER SANDWICH

2   slices of your favorite bread
      Chunky peanut butter

Vidalia Sweet Onion

Toast sliced bread. While still warm, spread chunky peanut butter so it will melt slightly. Then, place generous slice of Vidalia sweet onion on top of each slice of bread. Yields 2 sandwiches (for one person!)

Flo Broussard
Arlington, VA

PEANUT BUTTER AND ONION SANDWICH

Bread of your choice
Peanut butter

Mayonnaise
Vidalia Sweet Onion

Spread peanut butter on one slice of bread and mayonnaise on the other. Stack Vidalia Sweet Onion in the middle. Cut and enjoy.

"I know this sounds crazy. I learned it from my mother, and I didn't believe her until I tried it for myself"

J. Richard Lombardi
San Leandro, CA

Variation: Use salad dressing in place of mayonnaise.

Mrs. E. A. Patterson
Bloomsburg, PA

Variation: Substitute butter or margarine for mayonnaise.

Katherine H. Roe
Boynton Beach, FL

Variation: Omit mayonnaise.

June Sturgeon
Medford, MA

Don White
Aurora, CO

Variation: For easier handling, chop onion before placing on bread.

Mrs. H.C. Staylor
Princess Anne, MD

SUPER ONION SANDWICH

Pumpernickel bread	**Vidalia Sweet Onions, thinly sliced**
Mayonnaise	**Parsley, finely chopped**

Cut bread into rounds with biscuit cutter. Slice onions fairly thin to correspond to bread. Spread mayonnaise on 1 side of 2 slices of bread. Place onion between and spread mayonnaise all around outside edges. Roll sandwich in finely chopped parsley. Can be enjoyed whole or cut into ¼'s as hors d'oeuvre.

"This is my very favorite onion sandwich. Vidalias make it perfect."

Marie K. Andree
Rio Rancho, NM

TUNA SANDWICHES OR SALAD

1	6½-ounce can tuna fish, drained	¼	to ½ cup salad dressing or mayonnaise
½	cup chopped Vidalia Sweet Onions		Salt
			Pepper
1	cup chopped crisp apples, unpeeled		Lettuce
			Bread

Combine tuna fish, onions, apples and mayonnaise and stir until blended. Season with salt and pepper to taste. Spread between 2 sliced of bread. Top filling with lettuce. Yields 3 to 4 sandwiches.

"Arrange on lettuce leaf for salad. I use onions in almost everything I cook and your onions are the best. They have a wonderful flavor, easy to digest. So good!"

Mrs. Frankie Augustine
Glenwood Springs, CO

VIDALIA ONION SANDWICH

2	strips bacon	1	egg
1	sliced Vidalia Sweet Onion	1	slice good Cheddar cheese
	Salt	2	slices buttered bread
	Pepper		

Fry the bacon till crisp. Remove from pan. In the grease, sauté the onion. Salt and pepper gently. Shove aside and break an egg in the pan. Cover with a lid until set; top egg with cheese and re-cover the pan. When cheese has melted, slide egg and cheese onto 1 slice of buttered bread. Put the bacon strips on top, put onions over all and top with the other bread slice.
Yields 1 sandwich.

Helen H. Mitchell
Seattle, WA

VIDALIA/SCALI ONION SANDWICH

Scali bread, very thinly sliced	Salt
Mayonnaise	Pepper
Vidalia Sweet Onions, sliced very thinly	French dressing, non-creamy

Spread bread with mayonnaise. Place generous layer of sliced Vidalia sweet onions on one slice of bread. Salt and pepper lightly. Sprinkle French dressing over onions. Slice in finger portions.

"Scali bread is covered with sesame seeds. Buy directly from Italian bakery, if possible. Better make up a whole loaf–these sandwiches are addictive."

Clair F. Tetreault
Lincoln, MA

VIDALIA SWEET ONION GRILLED SANDWICH

2   slices Kosher-style seeded   2   slices Vidalia Sweet Onion
       rye bread per serving   per serving
2   slices Swiss cheese per serving   Margarine or butter

Butter rye bread on *outside*. Place 1 slice Swiss cheese on bread. Then 2 slices of Vidalia sweet onion. Then add the other slice of Swiss cheese. Pepper may be added if you wish. Put other slice of rye bread on top; place in frying pan and brown on top of stove using medium to low setting. Turn and brown other side. Cut and serve with sweet pickles and potato chips.

"This recipe does not work with ordinary yellow onions. Expand the size of your frying pan or griddle if making more than 1 sandwich or keep sandwiches warm in oven as you fry others."

Marguerite F. Garlick
Bowie, MD

Baked
&
Stuffed Treats

AMENDMENT TO "BLAND FAMILY FAVORITE"

1	Vidalia Sweet Onion, jumbo	1	chicken or beef bouillon cube
Butter		1	to 2 teaspoons garlic paste

Core Vidalia Sweet Onion. Season with salt and pepper. Add butter to one end and turn over. Place bouillon cube in center along with garlic paste. Top off with more butter to close hole. Wrap in foil and bake at 350 degrees for 30 to 40 minutes, or place directly on coals on the grill for 25 to 30 minutes. Turn numerous times so it will not burn. Serve 1 onion per person.

Jeff Berger
Springfield, MO

BAKED ONIONS A LA MODE

1	Vidalia Sweet Onion, peeled		Dash of pepper
1	teaspoon butter or margarine	1	teaspoon terriyaki or sweet
	Dash of salt		barbecue sauce

Slit top of onion criss-cross about ¼-inch deep. Place butter or margarine in the slit parts. Sprinkle with salt and pepper. Place sauce on top. Cover loosely and cook in microwave on high power approximately 5-6 minutes per onion. In conventional oven, preheat oven to 400 degrees. Place onion or onions in a shallow pan and heat about 15 minutes. One serving per onion.

"This recipe can be used as a snack or with a regular meal and can be used only with Vidalia Sweet Onions. I have used this recipe for over 3 years and is a favorite in my neighborhood and friends and relatives."

Bernard E. Meunier
Cumberland, RI

BAKED ONION WITH HERB BUTTER

½	cup butter or margarine	½	teaspoon dried leaf tarragon
½	teaspoon celery salt	4	Vidalia Sweet Onions
½	teaspoon parsley flakes		

Place butter or margarine in small bowl. Microwave at low or until softened. Add celery salt, parsley, and tarragon. Mix well. Set butter or margarine mixture aside at room temperature. Wash onions leaving outer skin intact. Trim top and bottom off each onion. Pierce onions deeply several times with a large fork. Wrap each onion in waxed paper twisting ends loosely to seal. Microwave at full power 9 to 11 minutes, until tender, turning onions over and rearranging once. Let stand wrapped 2 minutes. To serve top onions with herb-butter mixture. Serves 4.

"These onions make a tasty and attractive garnish for steak or roast platter."

Jennie A. Tarbell
Suffern, NY

BAKED VIDALIA ONION

1	Vidalia Sweet Onion	¼	teaspoon black pepper
1	tablespoon margarine	1½	tablespoons Parmesan cheese
¼	teaspoon salt		

Peel onion and quarter it about half way through. Put margarine down into cut. Sprinkle salt, pepper, and grated Parmesan cheese on top. Wrap in foil and bake at 350 degrees for 45 minutes. Yields 1 serving.

"Thanks to my brother-in-law, Bud Tarbell , for the introduction to Vidalia Onions"

Betty Jean Kitchens
Dadeville, AL

BAKED VIDALIA SWEET ONIONS

6	medium to large Vidalia Sweet Onions, peeled Butter		Garlic salt
		4	tablespoons Parmesan cheese

Peel the onions and place in a 9x13-inch baking pan lined with aluminum foil. Trim the tops off the onions slightly, so that a small pat of butter will sit on each onion. Sprinkle with garlic salt and top with Parmesan cheese. Cover and bake in 350 degree oven or grill 30 to 40 minutes or until soft. Yield 6 baked onions.

Leslie Prodonovich
Saugus, CA

BAKED VIDALIA SWEET ONIONS WITH RICE

7½	cups chopped Vidalia Sweet Onions	5	cups boiling water, salted
4	tablespoons butter	¾	cup grated Swiss cheese
½	cup raw rice	⅔	cup half & half

Sauté onions in butter until transparent. Cook rice in water for 5 minutes; drain and mix with onions. Add cheese and cream. Bake uncovered at 350 degrees for 1 hour. Serves 8.

Judy Lewis
Gaithersburg, MD

Evelyn Vannice
Grants Pass, OR

Mrs. Marlin F. Cole
Paradise Valley, AZ

Mrs. Deborah Brooks
Charlotte, NC

BAKED VIDALIA WITH BROWN SUGAR

4	large Vidalia Sweet Onions	¾	cup brown sugar
¼	pound butter or margarine	1	pint sour cream

Peel Vidalia sweet onions and mark top with a small cut X. Place in a pan or baking dish with sides at least 1-inch or more. In saucepan, melt butter, add brown sugar and stir in sour cream. Mix well. Pour over onions. Bake uncovered in 350 degree oven for 1 hour or until done to your taste.

"For more than 4 large Vidalias, double mixture. So good with noodles, pasta or angel hair."

Betty Roberts
Maywood, NJ

BAKED VIDALIAS AND PEANUTS

4	large Vidalia Sweet Onions	1	teaspoon black pepper
¼	cup crunchy peanut butter	3	tablespoons heavy cream
¼	cup shelled peanuts, roasted		

Peel the onions and trim the bottoms so that they will stand. Place them in a pan of hot water and boil them for 5 minutes until soft but not mushy. In a bowl, mix the remaining ingredients together. When the Vidalias are cooked, drain them and carefully make a hollow in each one. Stuff the hollows with the peanut mixture and place on a baking sheet. Bake in a 400 degree oven for 10 minutes. Serve hot. Serves 4.

Dot at Braswells

BAKED VIDALIA SWEETS

1	jumbo Vidalia Sweet Onion	1	beef bouillon cube
	Dash of salt	1	tablespoon butter
	Dash of pepper		

Core onion. Fill hollow with salt, pepper, bouillon cube and butter. Wrap in foil and bake in 350 degree oven for 45 minutes or until desired tenderness. Do not overbake, as this may cause a tough texture. Makes 1 serving.

Martha P. Beale
Norfolk, VA

BAKED VIDALIAS WITH SWISS CHEESE

1	medium Vidalia Sweet Onion, chopped	8	ounces Swiss cheese, shredded
		2	big dollops of mayonnaise

In a microwave or oven proof 2 quart dish mix onions and cheese together. Add enough mayonnaise to make into tuna fish consistency. Cover and bake in oven at 350 degrees for 30 minutes or bake in microwave on high for 8 minutes. Stirring occasionally. Serve hot with a spoon to dish onto crackers. Serves 20.

Linda Borschuk
Phoenix, MD

BAKED VIDALIAS WITH PARMESAN

	Herb seasoning to taste	½	cup grated Parmesan cheese
	Vegetable cooking spray	⅔	cup corn flake crumbs
5	Vidalia Sweet Onions, peeled, halved, and thinly sliced		

Spray a 9x13-inch baking pan with cooking spray. Scatter onions in pan and sprinkle with herb seasoning. Top with Parmesan cheese and then corn flake crumbs. Cover pan with aluminum foil and bake in oven at 350 degrees for 45 minutes. Serves 6.

Paula Golding
Highlands Ranch, CO

BETTE'S BAKED ONIONS ~ FRENCH STYLE

4	large Vidalia Sweet Onions, sliced	1	cup milk
¾	cup butter, divided	1½	cups chicken broth
¼	cup all purpose flour	¼	cup Burgundy wine
½	teaspoon salt (if using canned broth, omit)	¾	pound Gruyère cheese, shredded
¼	teaspoon ground pepper or to taste	1	French bread baguette, sliced into ½-inch rounds
		4	tablespoons butter, melted

In large skillet, sauté onions in ½ cup butter over medium heat, stirring frequently. Cook until onions are transparent about 15 minutes. Transfer onions to buttered 2-quart shallow baking dish. Set aside. In large saucepan over low heat, melt remaining 4 tablespoons butter. Whisk in flour and stir 2 minutes. Add salt, pepper, milk and chicken broth, stirring constantly until thickened. Stir in Burgundy. Pour sauce over onions. Sprinkle with cheese. Dip one side of bread slices in 4 tablespoons melted butter. Place slices buttered side up over sauce covering completely. Bake at 350 degrees for 30 minutes or until bread is completely browned. Serves 6 to 8.

Bette M. Holmber
Portsmouth, RI

BIG BAKED ONIONS

Vidalia Sweet Onions, good sized	Salt
Butter	Pepper

Preheat oven to 375 degrees. Do not wash or peel onions. Place onions on a foil lined sheet pan. Bake for 1 hour or until soft when pressed. Keep warm until ready to serve. Then slit tops and crown with butter, salt, and pepper. Serve 1 large onion per person.

Thorneta Rowe
Boyne City, MI

CREAMED VIDALIA ONIONS

4	cups sliced Vidalia Sweet Onions	4	tablespoons all purpose flour
2	tablespoons sweet unsalted butter	2	cups half & half, at room temperature
	Salt	½	teaspoon salt
4	tablespoons sweet unsalted butter		Ground nutmeg, optional
			Cayenne pepper, optional
			Grated Cheddar cheese, optional

Sauté onions in 2 tablespoons butter until crisp-tender. Season carefully with a small amount of salt. Set aside. In a large heavy saucepan, melt 4 tablespoons butter. Add flour and cook over medium-low heat for 3 to 4 minutes, stirring constantly. Add half & half and cook over medium heat until thick and bubbly, stirring constantly. Season with salt. Add onions and heat through seasoning carefully with a few grains of nutmeg and cayenne pepper, if desired.

Variation: Pour creamed onions into a buttered 1½-quart casserole dish, top with grated Cheddar cheese and bake at 375 degrees for 15 minutes, until cheese is bubbly. Serves 6.

"Everybody loves my Creamed Vidalias!"

Claudia Schlottman
Macon, GA

HONEY BAKED VIDALIAS

6	medium Vidalia Sweet Onions, (about 1½-inches peeled and halved crosswise	¼	cup honey
		2	tablespoons oleo, cut into small pieces
			Chopped parsley, to garnish

Arrange onions, cut side up, in an 11x7-inch microwave safe baking dish. Pour honey over top of onions and dot with oleo. Cover loosely with waxed paper. Microwave on high 8 to 10 minutes, basting with pan juice and rotating dish ¼ turn twice, until onions are tender. Serves 12.

Note: For garnish, sprinkle with chopped parsley.

Corinne Holm
Crystal Falls, MI

JANE'S BAKED ONIONS

2	to 3 large Vidalia Sweet Onions	½	cup skim milk
2	tablespoons butter, margarine or oil	1	teaspoon Worcestershire sauce
2	cups or 8-ounces Swiss cheese, grated	¼	teaspoon pepper
1	10-ounce can cream of chicken soup, undiluted	6	to 8 slices French bread, top side buttered

In a large skillet, cook onion rings in butter until tender but still white/transparent. Arrange onions in greased 1½-quart baking dish; sprinkle cheese on top. Blend soup, milk, Worcestershire sauce and pepper. Pour over cheese and onions and mix lightly. Arrange bread slices with buttered side up over top. This may be cooked on the grill with the cover closed or baked in the oven at 350 degrees for 30 minutes. Serves 4 to 6.

Jane Gorman
Ambler, PA

JUDITH'S BAKED ONIONS

4	Vidalia Sweet Onions	Pepper to taste
2	tablespoons butter or margarine	1 beef bouillon cube
Salt to taste		¼ cup water
		Grated Parmesan cheese, if desired

Place whole, trimmed onions in greased casserole dish. Place ½ tablespoon butter on top of each onion. Sprinkle salt and pepper on top of each. Dissolve bouillon cube in ¼ cup water and pour around the onions. Bake for 45 minutes in a 350 degree oven. Serve in small bowls. Top with grated Parmesan cheese if desired. Serves 4.

Judith N. Murray
Bethesda, MD

JUNE'S SWEET ONIONS

4	large Vidalia Sweet Onions	¾	stick butter or oleo cut up
½	cup brown sugar		

Cut onions in quarters and boil for 15 minutes in very little water. Drain well. Put onions into baking dish with sugar and butter and mix well. Cover with foil and bake in 350 degree oven for 30 to 45 minutes.

June Lowe
Round Pond, ME

MARTHA'S BAKED VIDALIA ONIONS

4	large Vidalia Sweet Onions	Black pepper
1	stick butter or margarine	

Slice onions and place in bottom of casserole dish. Put a pat of butter and black pepper on each onion. Add layers until dish is full. Cover with foil and bake in 400 degree oven for 30 to 40 minutes. Serves 4.
Note: Delicious served with vegetables and corn bread.

Martha Welch
Oakman, AL

VIDALIA SWEET ONION BAKE

Vidalia Sweet Onions, 1 per person	1	drop Tabasco sauce	
1	teaspoon butter	Dash of salt	
2	tablespoons soy sauce	Pinch of oregano	

Peel and core onions. Put in pan of ice water until they open. Place each onion on a piece of foil. Put 1 teaspoon of butter, 2 tablespoons soy sauce, 1 drop Tabasco, dash of salt, and a pinch of oregano on each onion. Wrap in foil and bake in 375 degree oven for 15 to 30 minutes.

Peter Lind
Novato, CA

ONIONS CALABRÉSE
(Italy)

3 to 4 large Vidalia Sweet Onions, peeled and sliced
3 garlic cloves, minced
3 tablespoons virgin olive oil
2 green peppers (banana), sliced thin
2 red bell peppers, sliced
2 tablespoons tomato paste
3 teaspoons red wine
Oregano
Salt and pepper
Dry red pepper flakes
Romano cheese to taste

Sauté the onions and garlic in the oil until tender. Add peppers and sauté a few minutes more. Stir in all remaining ingredients except cheese. Place in a small deep baking dish or casserole and top with cheese. Bake at 375 degrees for 45 minutes. Serves 6 as a side dish.
Note: Great with roast beef or steak.

Nancy Gnoli
Hartford, CT

SIMPLY BAKED SWEET VIDALIA

Vidalia Sweet Onion (1 per person)
1 tablespoon margarine per onion or to taste
Lemon and herb spice, to taste
½ teaspoon fresh chopped parsley

Cut both ends off the onion and peel. Core the center out of the top of the onion. Put margarine in the center of onion along with an abundant amount of lemon and herb spice. Stick cored out center back into top of onion. It will stick up like a satellite dish! For a whimsical touch - tilt it to one side! Cover with copious amount of lemon and herb spice again all over. Sprinkle with parsley. Bake at 350 degrees for 20 to 25 minutes depending on size of onion. Do not overbake. Yields 1 onion per person.
Note: Great dish for steak, chicken, pork chops, or fish.

W. C. Brewer, Jr.
Baltimore, MD

THE TEASE OF SPRING

6 medium Vidalia Sweet Onions, unpeeled
¼ cup olive oil
 Kosher (coarse) salt and freshly ground black pepper to taste
⅓ cup balsamic vinegar
⅓ cup fresh orange juice
2 teaspoons grated orange zest

Preheat oven to 375 degrees. Rub the skins of the onions generously with olive oil. Place them in a heatproof roasting pan and sprinkle with salt and pepper. Roast the onions until soft and tender, 45 to 60 minutes. Cut the onions in half through the root ends and arrange cut sides up on a serving platter. Add the vinegar and orange juice and zest to drippings in the roasting pan. Place the pan over medium-high heat and cook the liquid until reduced to a glaze. Drizzle the glaze over the roasted onions. Serve onions at room temperature. Serves 4 to 6.

Joseph and Mary Noonan
Norfolk, MA

SWEET & SOUR ONIONS

5 large Vidalia Sweet Onions
½ cup melted butter
½ cup boiling water
¼ cup cider vinegar
½ cup brown sugar

Slice onions and arrange in large lightly greased dish. Mix the rest of the ingredients and pour over onions. Cover and bake at 300 degrees for 1 hour.

Maxine Ours
Butler, MO

VIDALIA ONION AND TOMATO BAKE

6	large roma/Italian style tomatoes	½	teaspoon black pepper
1	large Vidalia Sweet Onion	½	cup fresh bread crumbs
1	teaspoon fresh dill	3	diced cloves garlic
1	teaspoon fresh thyme	1	cup Mozzarella cheese, grated
¼	teaspoon salt	¼	cup olive oil

Preheat oven to 350 degrees. Butter an 8-inch casserole. Blanch tomatoes to remove skin; core and cut into wedges. Turn upside down on paper towel to drain. Peel and slice onion into ¼-inch rings. Mix herbs, salt, pepper, and bread crumbs together. Layer ½ of the tomatoes and onions in casserole and top with ½ of garlic cloves. Sprinkle half of the crumb mixture over the tomatoes and onions along with half of the cheese. Drizzle with ½ of the olive oil. Repeat this ending with olive oil. Bake for 50 minutes or until bubbly. You want the onion to be still crisp and tender. Serves 6.

Note: For a more spicy dish add ½ to 1 teaspoon of red pepper flakes to herb/crumb mixture. If the plum style tomatoes are not available regular tomatoes may be substituted. Use 3 large or 6 small tomatoes depending on size.

Mrs. Sterling Sasser
Austin, TX

ONIONS STUFFED WITH SAUSAGE

2	large Vidalia Sweet Onions	¼	cup milk
1	pound bulk sausage meat	1	egg
½	cup bread crumbs	2	tablespoons snipped parsley

Preheat oven to 375 degrees. Peel onions. Cut them into halves, crosswise. Remove center rings and leave a hole approximately 1-inch in diameter. Combine remaining ingredients and blend well. Stuff onions with enough of the sausage mixture so that it makes a mound. Arrange the onions in a greased baking dish and bake until the sausage is cooked throughly and the onions are tender, about 20 minutes. Serves 4.

A Friend

STUFFED BAKED ONIONS

6   large Vidalia Sweet Onions
1   6-ounce box cornbread
      stuffing mix

2   cups or 8-ounces shredded
      sharp Cheddar cheese

Peel onions. Cut a small slice from top and bottom. Discard. Score each onion, making 6 wedges and cutting to within ½-inch of bottom. Prepare stuffing mix according to package directions. Cool. Stir in cheese. Fill onions with stuffing mixture. Wrap each onion in foil and place in a 9x13x2-inch baking pan. Bake at 350 degrees for 1 hour. Serves 6.

Dorothy B. Morgan
Oakmont, PA

STUFFED ONIONS

2   Vidalia Sweet Onions
1   9-ounce can peas, drained
1   4-ounce can sliced
        mushrooms, drained
½   teaspoon chicken granules

⅓   cup water
      Salt, to taste
      Pepper, to taste
¼   teaspoon thyme

Cut onions in half and hollow out, leaving bottom intact. Place in microwave-safe dish. Stuff with peas and mushrooms. Dissolve chicken granules in ⅓-cup water and pour over peas and mushrooms. Add salt, pepper and thyme. Microwave 7 to 9 minutes, turning after 4 minutes. Serves 4.
Note: This recipe makes a very nice presentation and is delicious.

Flo Jones
Royersford, PA

WHOLE VIDALIAS WITH SWEET PEA DRESSING

Cover Recipe

Vidalia Sweet Onions,
  peeled and cored
10 oz. box of frozen sweet
  peas

½ to 1 cup sour cream (depends
    on desired consistancy)
1   to ½ teaspoon sugar (to taste)

Drop onions in boiling water for 5 minutes or until as tender as desired. Drain while preparing dressing. Drop in frozen peas in same water, cook as per directions on box. Mix sour cream and sugar and gently fold in drained peas. Place onions on platter and fill cores with dressing. Garnish with fresh herbs of your choice.

Rosalind Harrold
Bainbridge, GA

BROCCOLI, CORN, ONION CASSEROLE

1   pound fresh broccoli
1   can cream style corn
1   egg
½ cup chopped Vidalia Sweet
      Onion

  Salt, to taste
  Pepper, to taste
1   cup seasoned crouton cubes
⅓ cup melted butter or marga-
      rine

Peel stems and chop broccoli. Parboil 5 minutes. Stir egg into corn, combine with onion, broccoli, salt and pepper. Toss cubes in melted butter. Mix ½ of cubes into broccoli mixture and sprinkle remaining cubes on top. Bake uncovered in 350 degree oven for 45 minutes. Serves 6 to 8.
Note: For low sodium diet, omit salt. This tastes better with butter rather than margarine.

Helen Larsgaarp
Hoyt Lakes, MN

Casseroles
&
Soufflès

B L A N D   F A R M S

BAKED CABBAGE LASAGNA

1	to 2 tablespoons olive oil	Basil, to taste	
3	to 4 Vidalia Sweet Onions	Parsley, to taste	
2	bell peppers	Oregano, to taste	
4	to 6 ounces mushrooms, (canned or bottled) drained	1	6-ounce can tomato paste
1	head cabbage	1	28-ounce can whole tomatoes or sauce
1	cup white wine, optional	1	pound any small pasta, elbow, shells, etc.
2	to 3 cups water		
Salt, to taste		½	to 1 pound Mozzarella cheese
Pepper, to taste		½	cup grated Parmesan cheese
Thyme, to taste			

Cut and dice all vegetables to about 1 square inch. Preheat oven to 350 degrees. In large 8-quart pot, heat olive oil. Sauté onions, peppers and mushrooms till golden brown. Add cabbage and wine, one cup water and the seasonings of your choice. If wine is not used, add more water. Bring to a boil and slow steam, stirring occasionally until vegetables reduce, about, 10 minutes. Add tomato paste, tomatoes and enough water to cover. Continue cooking until all vegetables are tender, about 30 minutes. Sample and adjust seasonings to taste. Slice Mozzarella into thin slices and set aside. Cook pasta 'al dente'; time this to be ready with vegetables. Drain. Combine drained pasta with vegetables. If too stiff, add tomato sauce; if too runny, add bread crumbs or flour. Place about ½-inch layer of vegetable-pasta mixture in a lightly greased 12x16-inch baking pan and spread evenly. Sparsely cover with part of the Mozzarella. Sprinkle Parmesan on uncovered areas. Continue alternating layers of mixture and cheese until finished. End with at least some Mozzarella cheese on each 2x3-inch portion. Sprinkle with remaining Parmesan cheese over top. Bake uncovered about 25-30 minutes in 350 degree oven until well warmed throughout. Cheese should be visibly melted on top. May be served immediately, but a short rest will ease portioning. Garnish with parsley, basil or oregano. Serves 12 to 16.

"A tasty, meatless casserole having unlimited variations. This recipe will keep at least a week refrigerated. Portions may be individually plastic wrapped and kept frozen indefinitely. Reheat in microwave. Except for cabbage and onions, this dish has no set ingredients. Using any 'leftover' pasta and almost any other vegetable is recommended. Variations might include white or wild rice, carrots, celery, etc. Use vegetable mix without any pasta for filler when using the standard lasagna-type pasta."

Monica Popko
Carrollton, TX

BAKED ONION CASSEROLE

6	Vidalia Sweet Onions, thinly sliced	Red pepper, taste	
½	pound mild Cheddar cheese	2	10¾-ounce can cream of mushroom soup, undilut
1	3¾-ounce package potato chips, crushed	¼	cup milk

Butter 9x13-inch baking dish. Layer alternately in thin layers onions, ch potato chips and pepper. Combine soup and milk in bowl and blend wel Pour over ingredients in baking dish. Bake 1 hour in 350 degree oven. Serves 8.
Note: More Vidalia sweet onions may be added to recipe if desired.

Mimi Guidry
Scott, LA

BAKED RICE AND MUSHROOM CASSEROLE

1	cup rice, uncooked	4	tablespoons butter
1	medium size Vidalia Sweet Onion, chopped	1	pound mushrooms, sliced
		Salt and pepper	

Cook rice according to package directions. Sauté onions in butter. Add mushrooms and cook 10 minutes. Mix onions and mushrooms with rice and seasonings. Bake in 350 degree oven for 30 minutes. Serves 6.

"I have used this recipe for over 50 years."

Edna Ewen
Lubbock, TX

BROCCOLI AND ONION CASSEROLE

2   to 3 cups Vidalia Sweet
    Onions, sliced in small pieces
2   10-ounce packages frozen
    broccoli
2   tablespoons butter
2   tablespoons all purpose flour
    Salt

    Pepper
⅔   cup milk
1   3-ounce package cream
    cheese
½   cup dry white wine
    Toasted and sliced almonds

Boil onions in lightly salted water until barely done. Repeat the same process with the broccoli. Drain both. For sauce, melt butter in saucepan, add flour, salt, and pepper. Blend milk in slowly. Add cream cheese. Stir until smooth. Remove from heat and add wine. Place broccoli and onions in 1½-quart casserole. Cover with sauce. Bake uncovered in 350 degree oven for 30 minutes. When ready to serve, sprinkle almonds on top. Serves 8.

Anne W. Schumacher
Augusta, ME

CARROT - ONION CASSEROLE

1   large bunch carrots, cooked
    and sliced
1   cup chopped Vidalia Sweet
    Onion
1   cup shredded Cheddar cheese

1   stick butter or margarine,
    melted
1   tube round buttery flavored
    crackers, crushed

Mix all ingredients together gently. Put in lightly greased casserole dish. Top with cracker crumbs. Bake uncovered in 350 degree oven for 40 minutes.
Serves 4 to 6.

"Even carrot haters will love this. This recipe always gets raves!"

Mary Terese Walsh
Chicago, IL

CEBOLA CASSEROLE

	Potatoes, sliced ¼-inch thick	Butter
	Flour	Milk
1	to 2 large Vidalia Sweet	Salt, to taste
	Onions, sliced ¼-inch thick	Pepper, to taste
	Ham, cut in¼ to ½-inch cubes	Garlic, to taste

Grease 2x9x13-inch pan. Put 1 layer of potatoes, sprinkle with flour and a few pats butter. Put a layer of onions, sprinkle with flour . Layer potatoes again and sprinkle with flour and butter. Then a layer of ham, potatoes, onions, then potato layer again. Lightly season each layer. Top layer should be about ½-inch below top of pan. Pour in milk to bottom of last layer of potatoes. Bake at 350 degrees for about 1 hour. Serves 4 as a main dish and 10 as a side dish.

"Cebola is Portuguese for onion. For variation, put croutons or bread crumbs between layers."

Carl W. Boutilier
Block Island, RI

CHEESY HAM'N BEAN CASSEROLE

2	tablespoons butter	8	to 10 slices Cheddar cheese
2	tablespoons flour	1	package frozen cut green
2	cups milk		beans(10 oz), defrost just
5	slices Cheddar cheese		enough to separate
3	cups cubed ham	1	large Vidalia Sweet Onion,
3	medium potatoes, thinly		sliced thinly
	sliced		Salt, to taste
			Pepper, to taste

Melt butter and make paste with flour. Add milk and cut up cheese. Cook stirring constantly over medium heat until sauce thickens. Set aside. Cut up ham, potatoes and cheese; separate Vidalia sweet onion slices into rings and open package of frozen cut green beans. Using a 2-quart casserole dish, layer potatoes, salt, pepper, onion rings, green beans, ham, cheese and pour cheese sauce over layer completely. Repeat layering twice. Bake covered in 350 degree oven for 1½-hours. Serves 4.

Betty Muench
Carefree, AZ

CHERYL'S VIDALIA ONION CASSEROLE

1	stick margarine or butter	2	eggs
4	medium Vidalia Sweet Onions, sliced	½	to 1 cup milk
			Salt, to taste
12	saltine crackers, crushed		Pepper, to taste
1	10¾-ounce can cream of mushroom soup, undiluted		Grated Cheddar cheese

Melt margarine or butter and cook onions until tender. Butter casserole dish and line dish with cracker crumbs. Add onions and soup in layers. Beat eggs and add milk, salt and pepper. Pour over casserole. Sprinkle cheese and a few more cracker crumbs over top. Bake at 350 degrees until brown and bubbly. Serves 4 to 6.

Cheryl Van Ness
Marietta, GA

CHICKEN AND VIDALIA ONION CASSEROLE

1	large Vidalia Sweet Onion	1	10¾-ounce can cream of chicken soup, undiluted
2	boneless and skinless chicken breasts		

Cut onion in half crosswise and put in small casserole dish. Place chicken breasts on top of onion. Spoon undiluted chicken soup over chicken. Cover and bake 1 hour at 350 degrees. Let set a few minutes for flavors to blend. Serve with noodles. Serves 2.

Ruth Coleman
Orlando, FL

CORN CASSEROLE

2   16½-ounce cans cream style corn
1   cup chopped Vidalia Sweet Onion
1   cup sour cream
1   stick oleo, melted
1   8½-ounce box sweetened corn muffin mix
2   eggs, beaten

Blend all ingredients together well. Pour into a well greased 2-quart casserole dish and bake for 1 hour in 350 degree oven. Serves 12.

Virginia N. Strating
Fulton, IL

DIXIE'S VIDALIA CASSEROLE

3   to 4 Vidalia Sweet Onions, sliced thin
1   10¾-ounce can cream of chicken or cream of mushroom soup, undiluted
½   soup can of milk
1   tablespoon soy sauce
    Pepper
¼   pound grated Swiss cheese French bread, sliced, quartered and buttered

Heat oven to 350 degrees. Sauté onions in small amount of butter until yellow and soft. Blend and heat soup, soy sauce, milk and pepper. Place onions in ungreased 1½-quart shallow baking dish. Place grated cheese on top of onions and then the soup mixture. Place quartered buttered bread on top. Bake uncovered 30 minutes in 350 degree oven. Serves 6.

Mrs. Neill W. MacArthur
Jasper, GA

EASY CASSEROLE

½   pound ground beef
1   medium Vidalia Sweet Onion,
     sliced
4   medium potatoes, sliced

1   10¾-can cream of celery
     soup, undiluted

Brown ground beef in skillet. Drain grease. Layer meat, onions and potatoes in casserole dish. Put soup on top of layers. Cover and bake at 325 degrees for 1½ to 2 hours. Serves 3.

Kay Repshire
Russell Springs, KS

ETHEL'S VIDALIA ONION CASSEROLE

4   large Vidalia Sweet Onions,
     thickly sliced to 1½-inches
½   cup or 1 stick butter or
     margarine
⅔   cup chicken broth
⅓   cup sherry

2   tablespoons all purpose flour
1½   cups soft bread crumbs
½   cup grated sharp Cheddar
     cheese
2   tablespoons grated Parmesan
     cheese

Sauté onions in butter or margarine until transparent. Add chicken broth, sherry and flour. When slightly thickened, transfer to medium sized casserole dish. Top with crumbs and both cheeses. Bake uncovered at 350 degrees for about 20 minutes or until lightly browned and bubbly. Serves 4 to 6.

Ethel Johnson
Brookline, MA

GEORGIA CASSEROLE

8	strips bacon	⅓	of an 8-ounce package
2	large Vidalia Sweet Onions		Havarti or Swiss cheese
1	stick margarine		Parmesan grated cheese
4	large tomatoes		Italian seasonings
1	individual package club crackers		

Cook bacon and drain. Slice onions and sauté in margarine. Set aside. In a 9x13-inch casserole dish, layer half of the onions, bacon, tomatoes, and both cheeses. Make a second layer, sprinkling Italian seasonings on top. Bake uncovered 45 minutes at 350 degrees. Let sit for 10 minutes and then cut into squares.
Serves 8.

Elizabeth Patten
Elbridge, NY

GLADYS' CASSEROLE

5	large Vidalia Sweet Onions, sliced or chopped		Seasoning salt Fresh ground pepper
1	stack round butter flavored crackers, crushed	1	cup shredded sharp Cheddar cheese
1	pound hot Italian sausage, browned and drained	1	4-ounce jar chopped pimentos, drained
1	10¾-ounce can cream of mushroom soup, undiluted		

Put half the onions in 12x17-inch casserole. Sprinkle on cracker crumbs and then sausage. Add the rest of the onions. Spread soup over top. Salt and pepper to taste. Add grated cheese and sprinkle with pimentos. Bake uncovered in 400 degree oven for 50 minutes. Serves 6 to 8.

Janet W. Martin
Prescott, AZ

GRANDMA HENNY'S CASSEROLE

1	pound bacon	4	to 6 ounces thin spaghetti, broken in half
1	green pepper, large diced		
1	to 2 large Vidalia Sweet Onions, large diced	1	28-ounce can stewed tomatoes Buttered bread crumbs, optional

Cut bacon into ¼-inch pieces. Dice onion and green pepper. Simmer bacon, onion, and green pepper together until onion is translucent and green pepper soft. Cook spaghetti. Combine with bacon mixture and tomatoes. Place in 9x13-inch pan. Top with buttered bread crumbs, if desired. If casserole is too dry, add a little tomato sauce to the mixture. Bake uncovered in 350 degree oven for 30-45 minutes. Serves 10.

Wava Hawker
Perrysburg, OH

HAWAIIAN ONIONS

4	large Vidalia Sweet Onions, peeled	½	teaspoon Worcestershire sauce
1	15-ounce can corned beef hash	6	slices canned pineapple, drained
1	tablespoon brown sugar	2	tablespoons melted butter
½	teaspoon dry mustard		

Preheat oven to 400 degrees. Grease a 12x8x2-inch baking dish. Cook whole onions in boiling water until tender crisp, approximately 30 minutes. Slice top off each onion and remove center. Chop sufficient to make 1 cup. While onions are cooking, mix corned beef hash, brown sugar, mustard and Worcestershire sauce together and add the 1 cup of chopped onions. Fill each onion with mixture. Arrange 4 slices of pine-apple in baking dish and top each slice with stuffed onion. Place ½ slice pineapple on top of each onion and brush with melted butter. Bake in preheated oven for 40 minutes. Baste once or twice with pan juices during cooking. Serves 4.

"This is one of my family's favorite dishes."

Fran Hall
Butler, MO

HEAVENLY VIDALIAS

2	large Vidalia Sweet Onions	½	cup milk
2	tablespoons butter	1	tablespoon soy sauce
¼	teaspoon pepper	1	cup buttered fresh bread crumbs
½	pound shredded Swiss cheese		
1	10¾-ounce can cream of mushroom soup, undiluted		

Peel and slice Vidalia sweet onions thinly. Separate slices into rings and sauté in 2 tablespoons butter until transparent. Sprinkle the ¼ teaspoon pepper over onions. Place sautéed onions in casserole dish and cover with cheese. In a separate bowl, combine soup, milk and soy sauce and pour over onions and cheese. Top with buttered bread crumbs. Bake uncovered at 350 degrees for 40 minutes. Serves 6 to 8.

"This is a wonderful accompaniment for beef or pork. Since soy sauce and canned soups tend to be on the salty side, I do not add salt to this recipe."

Beverly Stewart Barter
Hyannis, MA

HONEYED ONIONS

8	Vidalia Sweet Onions, peeled	3	tablespoons honey
3	tablespoons butter		Pinch of salt, if desired
4	tablespoons tomato juice		

Peel and half Vidalia sweet onions. Melt butter and mix with honey and tomato juice. Lay onions in buttered casserole dish. Pour butter mixture over onions and bake uncovered in 350 degree oven for 1 hour and 15 minutes. Serves 4 to 6.

Janice Lepisko
Brownsville, VT

ITALIAN SAUSAGE, ONIONS AND POTATO CASSEROLE

1	pound Italian sausage	1	large bell pepper, cut into
2	large red potatoes, leave		large cubes
	skins on; cut into eighths	1	package dry Italian salad
2	large Vidalia Sweet Onions,		dressing mix ·
	cut into large cubes		

Cut sausage into 2-inch pieces. Place in casserole dish with potatoes, onions and pepper. Sprinkle with dry salad dressing mix and toss gently. Place cover on casserole and bake 1 hour at 400 degrees. Let sit about 10 minutes for flavors to blend. Serves 4.

Ruth Coleman
Orlando, FL

JODY'S VIDALIA ONION CASSEROLE

1½	cups corn muffin mix	½	stick margarine
1	egg, beaten	1	cup sour cream
1	15-ounce can cream style	½	cup grated sharp Cheddar
	corn		cheese
⅓	cup milk	¼	teaspoon salt
1	large Vidalia Sweet Onion		

Combine muffin mix, egg, cream style corn, and milk together and pour into a buttered casserole dish. Sauté onion in margarine. Add sour cream, cheese and salt to onions and pour on top of the cornbread mixture. Bake uncovered at 350 degrees for 40 to 45 minutes.

Jody Tindall
Frankfort, IN

LAYERED VIDALIA SWEET ONION CASSEROLE

3   Vidalia Sweet Onions, sliced
1   to 2 tablespoons butter
1   10¾-ounce can cream of
      chicken soup, undiluted
1   cup grated Swiss cheese
1   loaf French bread, buttered

Cook onions in butter until soft. Put in casserole dish. Spread chicken soup, undiluted, over onions. Layer grated cheese over top. Top with slices of buttered French bread. Bake uncovered in 350 degree oven for 30 minutes.
Serves 8 to 10.

Elinor Butman
Temple Hills, MD

LIP-SMACKING VIDALIA SWEET ONION CASSEROLE

5   cups sliced Vidalia Sweet
      Onions
6   tablespoons butter or marga-
      rine
½   cup self-rising flour
¼   teaspoon black pepper
½   teaspoon salt
1   teaspoon ground cumin
3   cups grated sharp Cheddar
      cheese, divided

Parboil onions in a little water or soften in microwave. Drain well. Melt butter or margarine over onions. Sprinkle flour, pepper, salt, and cumin over mixture and stir to mix well. Stir in ½ to 1 cup cheese. Spray 8x12-inch pan with cooking spray. Spread onion mixture evenly. Sprinkle remaining cheese over top. Bake uncovered at 350 degrees for 30 minutes.

Alice Hawley
Warner Robins, GA
Third Place Winner
Georgia National Fair

ONION CASSEROLE

4	large Vidalia Sweet Onions, cut into rings	½	cup cracker crumbs
	Salted water to cover	¼	cup melted butter or oleo
1	10¾-ounce can cream of celery soup, undiluted		

Peel and slice onions. Cover with salted water and cook for 5 minutes. Drain. Add cream of celery soup and spoon into lightly greased casserole. Top with buttered cracker crumbs. Can be baked in a low oven with a roast, until on the dry side and well browned or in a high oven alone long enough to be well browned. Serves 6 to 8.

"Very good with almost any kind of entree."

Marian Cumps
Sun Lakes, AZ

ONION CASSEROLE WITH CORNBREAD STUFFING

4	cups Vidalia Sweet Onions, sliced	1	10¾-ounce can cream of mushroom soup, undiluted
½	cup butter or margarine	½	cup sour cream
1¼	cups cornbread stuffing mix		Buttered bread crumbs

Cook onions in butter until they are transparent. Combine with other ingredients and place in casserole dish. Top with buttered bread crumbs. Bake uncovered in 300 degree oven 45 - 60 minutes until brown.

Mrs. Clarence Peacock
Nashville, TN

ONION CASSEROLE WITH CAYENNE

5	jumbo Vidalia Sweet Onions, sliced	1½	cups sliced fresh mushrooms Salt
1	10¾-ounce can mushroom soup, undiluted	1	teaspoon cayenne pepper
1½	cups shredded Cheddar cheese	½	cup crumbled potato chips

Layer ingredients in a buttered 3-quart casserole dish. Layer first ½ of the sliced onions; then ½ of the mushroom soup; ½ of the cheese and all the sliced mushrooms. Sprinkle with ½ the cayenne pepper. Repeat layers using the remaining onions, mushroom soup, cheese and cayenne pepper. Top with crumbled potato chips. Bake uncovered at 350 degrees for 45-60 minutes or until onions are tender and casserole is golden and bubbly. Serves 6.

"You'll be surprised what the cayenne pepper does for the casserole."

Arlene Seybolt
Miami, OK

ONION CASSEROLE A LA TOMA

2	tablespoons butter	¾	cup cream
4	large Vidalia Sweet Onions	¾	cup water
⅓	pound ground pork	1	teaspoon salt
¼	pound ground veal	¼	teaspoon white pepper
⅓	pound bread crumbs	½	cup beef stock, or as needed

Melt butter in skillet and sauté onions until golden brown. Mix meats, bread crumbs, cream, and water until smooth. Season with salt and pepper. Cover bottom of casserole with ½ the onions. Spread meat on top of onions. Then spread with remaining onions. Pour some stock over mixture making holes so stock will run down. Bake uncovered in moderate 375 degree oven for 25 minutes. Cover if crust becomes too brown. Serve hot. Serves 6.

"Casserole should be as round as a 9-inch pie plate and at least 6-inches deep."

Florence M. Toma
Port Chester, NY

ONIONS CELESTE

6	to 8 large Vidalia Sweet Onions	½	to 1 can milk
4	tablespoons butter or margarine		Salt, to taste
			Pepper, to taste
½	pound American cheese		Croutons to garnish
1	10¾-ounce can cream of chicken soup, undiluted		

Peel and thinly slice onions and sauté in butter or margarine. Dice cheese and combine with soup, milk, salt, and pepper. Place onions in greased casserole. Pour the cheese mixture over the onions. Top with croutons. Bake uncovered 1/2 hour at 350 degrees. Serves 4.

"Serve over steamed cabbage, asparagus, broccoli, baked potatoes, noodles, rice, etc. - be creative. It's a delicious compliment to any meal."

Carol Knight
Halifax, PA

Variation: Use Swiss cheese in place of American and mushroom soup in place of chicken soup.

Anne Stine
Shermansdale, PA

ONION AND POTATO CASSEROLE

5	medium potatoes	1½	cups Cheddar cheese, grated divided
1½	cups sour cream		Salt
5	medium Vidalia Sweet Onions		Pepper

Boil potatoes with skin on. Cool and peel. Shred potatoes coarsely in large bowl. Thinly slice onions and add to sour cream. Fold into potatoes. Add ¾ the grated cheese, salt, and pepper to your taste. Mix well and place in 2½-quart buttered casserole. Sprinkle remaining cheese on top. Bake uncovered for 40 to 45 minutes in 350 degree oven. Serves 6.

Mrs. Angie Pirro
East Norwalk, CT

ONION CHEESE CASSEROLE

6	large Vidalia Sweet Onions, cut into ½ inch wedges	1	cup chopped scallions
¾	cup water	½	plus ¼ cup grated Parmesan cheese
3	cups shredded Cheddar cheese	1	garlic clove, minced
1	cup all purpose flour	¼	cup soft fresh bread crumbs

Preheat oven to 350 degrees. Combine onions and water in large saucepan. Cover and simmer 20 to 30 minutes, stirring occasionally. Drain. Combine in large bowl, cooked onions, cheddar cheese, flour, scallions, ½ cup Parmesan cheese, and garlic. Place in greased 2-quart casserole dish. Mix together the remaining ¼ cup Parmesan and bread crumbs and sprinkle over onion mixture. Bake uncovered for 35 minutes or until top turns golden brown. Serve with meat, chicken, fish, etc.. Serves 8.

Sherry Letsch
Glendale, AZ

ONION AND DILL CASSEROLE

2	cups diced Vidalia Sweet Onions	1	cup cottage cheese
2	red peppers, diced	1	egg
1	clove garlic	⅓	cup chopped fresh dill
1	cup sliced mushrooms	⅓	cup parsley
3	tablespoons oil or 1 cup chicken stock	4	tablespoons Parmesan cheese, divided
2	cups cooked rice, brown and white	⅓	cup bread crumbs
		1	tablespoons melted butter

Sauté onions, peppers, mushrooms, and garlic until limp in oil or stock. In bowl, fold together vegetables, rice, cottage cheese, egg, herbs, and 3 tablespoons Parmesan cheese. Pour into 9-inch buttered square pan. Combine 1 tablespoon Parmesan cheese, bread crumbs, and melted butter and sprinkle over casserole. Bake uncovered at 375 degrees for 30 minutes. Serves 4 to 6.

Alice Cheeseman
Unity, ME

ONION~TUNA~POTATO CASSEROLE

3	to 4 medium white potatoes, sliced	2	cups medium white sauce
1	6.5-ounce can tuna, drained	1	teaspoon salt
1	to 2 medium Vidalia Sweet Onions, chopped	½	teaspoon black pepper
		2	tablespoons butter

White Sauce:

2	tablespoons butter or margarine	2	cups milk
		1/4	cup all purpose flour

Melt butter. Stir in flour to form paste. Gradually add milk and cook over medium heat stirring constantly until thick.

Alternate layers. Layer sliced potatoes, tuna, and onions in casserole dish. Add salt, black pepper, and butter to white sauce. On each layer put a small amount of white sauce and pour the rest on top. Bake at 350 degrees for 1 hour. Serves 3 to 4.

Norma E. Jones
Decatur, IL

SAVORY VIDALIA ONIONS

2	pounds Vidalia Sweet Onions	1	teaspoon salt
½	teaspoon salt		Dash pepper
2	quarts water	1	cup chili sauce
½	cup brown sugar	1	ounce butter

Wash and peel onions. Slice, halve or leave whole. Add salt to water and bring to a boil. Add onions and reheat to boiling, reduce heat and simmer uncovered for 5 to 7 minutes. Drain. Arrange onions in baking dish. Combine remaining ingredients and pour over onions. Bake at 357 degrees until tender. Serves 6 to 8.

Winnie McClennen
Sellersville, PA

SAUSAGE AND RICE CASSEROLE

Cooking spray
2 large Vidalia Sweet Onions,
    sliced
1 pound sliced smoked turkey
    sausage
1 16-ounce can stewed tomatoes

3 cups cooked rice
   Salt, to taste
   Pepper, to taste
½ cup grated Cheddar cheese

Spray pan with cooking spray and sauté onions. Remove onions to large bowl. In same pan, brown sliced sausage. Mix onions, sausage, tomatoes and rice thoroughly. Season with salt and pepper to taste and pour into 2½ to 3 -quart casserole. Cover and bake in 350 degree oven for 45 minutes. Remove from oven and sprinkle cheese on top. Uncover and return to oven and bake for another 15 minutes. Serves 8.

Alice Henry
Fayetteville, NY

SOUBISE

½ cup rice
6 tablespoons butter
2 tablespoons oil
2 pounds Vidalia Sweet Onions

½ teaspoon salt
   Lemon juice
   Pepper

Pour boiling water on rice (enough to cover well). Boil 5 minutes. Drain. Peel and chop onions. Melt butter and oil in baking dish. Add onions, rice, and ½ teaspoon salt and mix to coat well. Cover baking dish and bake in 325 degree oven, stirring occasionally for about 1 hour until rice is completely cooked and onions are soft and golden. Add lemon juice, and salt and pepper to taste. Serves 6.

"Soubise is an old traditional French recipe which brings out the best in onions!"

Mrs. C. Minor Barringer
Chadds Ford, PA

SOUBISE WITH CHEESE

½ cup white rice
2 pounds Vidalia Sweet Onions
4 tablespoons butter
¾ teaspoons salt
¾ teaspoon pepper

4 tablespoons heavy cream
½ cup grated cheese, Swiss
   Cheddar or Monterey Jack
3 to 4 quarts boiling water,
   salted

Drop rice into boiling water and boil for exactly 5 minutes; drain. Peel and slice onions very thinly. Heat butter in large flame-proof casserole. Add onions and toss to coat evenly. Onions will cook down. Stir in rice, salt, and pepper. Cover casserole and bake in 300 degree oven for 1½-hours until rice and onions are very tender; stir occasionally. The mixture will turn a slight golden color. Mix in cream and cheese and adjust the seasoning. Serves 8.

"Served with both meat and fish."

Frances C. Gundrey
Santa Fe, NM

SUMMER CASSEROLE

2 medium zucchini, sliced ¼-inch
2 large tomatoes, sliced ¼-inch
2 large Vidalia Sweet Onions,
   thinly sliced

2 teaspoons Italian seasonings,
   or to taste
   Salt, to taste
   Pepper, to taste
4 thin slices Swiss cheese

Preheat oven to 350 degrees. In buttered 2-quart casserole, repeat layers of ingredients in order listed and ending with cheese. Bake at 350 degrees uncovered for 25 to 30 minutes or until vegetables are crisp and tender and cheese is melted and lightly brown. Serve with slotted spoon as some liquid may accumulate in bottom of dish. Recipe can be doubled. Serves 4.

"This is a simple, easily prepared casserole that makes a light one-dish meal. It also works well to balance a cold meal of chicken, tuna, or macaroni salad."

C. W. Williams
Englishtown, NJ

SWEET AND SOUR VIDALIAS

½ cup brown sugar   ½ cup butter or margarine
½ cup vinegar   6 whole Vidalia Sweet Onions

Put onions in oven proof casserole. Melt sugar, vinegar, and butter together over low heat and add to onions. Bake at 250 to 275 degrees for 2½ to 3 hours uncovered. Serves 6.

Georgia Jubitz
Hood River, OR

VIDALIA ONIONS AMADINE

2 large Vidalia Sweet Onions   1 teaspoon salt
8 whole cloves   ¼ teaspoon nutmeg
4 tablespoons butter   ⅛ teaspoon coriander
4 tablespoons sherry wine   ¼ teaspoon ginger
1 tablespoon honey   ⅓ cup almonds, slivered and
                                       lightly toasted in oven

Peel whole onions, removing as little as possible at each end. Cut each onion in half across so that the whole rings are facing up on each half. Put onions in skillet with about 1-inch water. Cover and simmer for 10 minutes. Drain onions on absorbent towels. Stick one whole clove in the center of each half onion. Place onions in a casserole dish with cover. Melt together in small saucepan the butter, sherry, honey, salt, nutmeg, coriander, and ginger. Pour the sauce over the onion halves, cover and bake at 325 to 350 degrees until just tender, about 30 minutes, basting with juices twice. Uncover the casserole, raise the heat, and reduce the sauce until slightly thickened. Sprinkle top with toasted, slivered almonds. Serves 4.

John David Ober
Brunswick, ME

VIDALIA ONION CASSEROLE

5 large Vidalia Sweet Onions	Parmesan cheese
1 stick oleo	
24 round butter flavored crackers, crushed	

Peel and slice onions and sauté in oleo. Put a layer of onions in casserole, then a layer of crushed crackers. Sprinkle the crackers with Parmesan cheese. Repeat another layer of onions, crackers and Parmesan cheese. Bake uncovered in 325 degree oven for 30 minutes uncovered.

Margery E. Arnold
Fredericksburg, VA

VIDALIA ONION/CHEESE CASSEROLE

1 pound Vidalia Sweet Onions, sliced and separated	1 teaspoon salt
1 egg, beaten	½ teaspoon pepper
1 cup cream, heavy or whipping cream	¾ to 1 cup shredded Cheddar cheese
	Paprika, for color and taste

Cover onions in a pot with enough water to cover. Bring to a boil and boil about 1 minute. Drain. Transfer to casserole dish, which has been sprayed with cooking spray. Combine beaten egg, cream, salt, and pepper. Pour over onions. Sprinkle with cheese and paprika. Bake uncovered 25 to 30 minutes at 350 degrees. Serves 6.

Bonnie Sampler
Richardson, TX
Mrs. George R. Ramel
Hopkinton, OH

VIDALIA ONION CHEESE STRATA

2	cups thinly sliced Vidalia Sweet Onions	2½	cups milk
8	slices bread	¼	teaspoon dry mustard
8	ounces sharp Cheddar cheese, sliced	3	drops hot red pepper sauce
3	eggs, beaten	1	teaspoon salt
		¼	teaspoon Worcestershire sauce
		2	tablespoons melted butter

Separate onion slices into rings. Trim crusts from bread. Place 4 slices bread in bottom of a buttered 9-inch square baking dish. Top with half the cheese and onions. Repeat. Combine beaten eggs, milk and seasonings. Pour over ingredients in baking dish. Cover and refrigerate several hours or overnight. Uncover. Drizzle with melted butter and bake in preheated 350 degree oven 50 to 60 minutes or until firm. Cut into squares to serve. Serves 6.

Patt Cameron
Claremore, OK

VIDALIA ONION PUDDING

2¼	pounds Vidalia Sweet Onions, halved and thinly sliced	4	eggs
3	tablespoons peanut oil	2	egg yolks
¼	cup bourbon	2	teaspoons lemon juice
2	garlic cloves, minced		Salt
1	cup heavy cream		Pepper
			Cayenne pepper

Cook onions in oil until golden brown, about 40 minutes. Stir in bourbon and garlic. Cook until liquid evaporates, cool. Blend cream, eggs, and yolks. Mix onions and lemon juice. Season with salt, pepper and cayenne pepper. Pour into ceramic baking dish. Bake in preheated 350 degree oven for 30 minutes. Serves 6.

Barbara Cover
Alexandria, VA

VIDALIA SWEET ONION CASSEROLE

1　jumbo or 2 medium Vidalia
　　Sweet Onions, sliced and
　　halved
1　10¾-ounce can cream of
　　mushroom soup, undiluted

Butter
Potato chips, crushed
Cheddar cheese
Paprika

Fill small casserole ⅓ full of onions. Add ⅓ can soup and continue to layer onions and soup. Dot with butter and cover with crushed potato chips, cheese and paprika. Bake in 350 degree oven for 1 hour. If it begins to brown too soon, cover lightly with foil. Serves 4.

Mrs. D. W. Bozeman
Pecos, TX

VIDALIA SWEET ONION SOUFFLÉ

1　tablespoon butter
1　tablespoon all-purpose flour
¼　teaspoon salt
1　cup milk
½　cup bread crumbs
1　teaspoon parsley

1　cup cold boiled Vidalia Sweet
　　Onions, chopped fine
1　egg yolk, beaten
2　egg whites
　　Paprika

Make white sauce from butter, flour, salt, and milk. Add to bread crumbs, parsley, Vidalia onion and beaten egg yolk. Beat egg whites until frothy and add to the onion mixture, folding in carefully. Pour into a buttered soufflé dish. Sprinkle with paprika. Bake in 350 degree oven for 15 minutes.
Serves 6.
Note: Serve with your favorite cream sauce.

Mrs. Logan D. Wilson
Greenville, TX

VIDALIA ONION SOUFFLÉ

5	large Vidalia Sweet Onions, chopped fine	2	tablespoons butter
1½	cups water	3	tablespoons cream
3	tablespoons butter	½	teaspoon salt
5	tablespoons all-purpose flour	½	cup chopped pecans
5	large eggs, separated		Sugar
5	tablespoons sugar		Parmesan cheese

In a heavy saucepan, put onions, butter and water. Cover with wax paper and secure lid. Steam until water is absorbed. Mash onions and add flour, egg yolks, 5 tablespoons sugar, 2 tablespoons butter, cream and salt. Beat egg whites until stiff and fold into onion mixture. Pour into buttered 9x5-inch Pyrex dish. Mix pecans with a little sugar and Parmesan cheese. Sprinkle over top. Bake uncovered in 350 degree oven until firm and lightly browned, about 30 minutes. Serves 8.

"At a buffet supper, recipe serves 8 or more but for a family gathering, it serves 6 generously."

Helen G. Richardson
Decatur, GA

Vegetables

&

Stir Fries

BAKED CORN~CHEESY ONIONS

8   medium Vidalia Sweet Onions
Instant beef bouillon
Salt and pepper, to taste
1   can cheese soup, undiluted

1   11-ounce can whole kernel
     corn, drained
1   2-ounce jar pimentos

Skin and prepare onions, hollowing out to the bottom center. Fill hole with ¼ teaspoon instant bouillon. Season with salt and pepper to taste. Put onions in greased pan with ½ cup water. Bake about 1 hour in regular oven, well covered. While onions are baking, pour cheese soup into double boiler, add corn, and pimentos. Heat well. When onions are done, place on platter and cover with cheese mixture. Serve immediately. Serves 8.

Mrs. Virgil E. Boyd
W. Sedona, AZ

MARINATED CARROTS

2   carrots, partially cooked
1   Vidalia Sweet Onion
1   green pepper
½   cup vinegar
½   cup sugar

½   cup oil
1   can tomato soup, undiluted
½   teaspoon salt
½   teaspoon pepper
½   teaspoon dry mustard

Slice partially cooked carrots quite thin. Slice onion thin. Dice green peppers. In saucepan combine vinegar, sugar, oil, tomato soup, salt, pepper and mustard. Bring to a boil and boil for 1 minute. Pour over vegetables. Stir and chill.
Note: They will keep for days in the refrigerator.

Betty Blake
Sequim, WA

COUNTRY CABBAGE

5	to 6 slices bacon	1	teaspoon salt
1	medium head fresh cabbage	¼	cup sugar
1	to 2 large Vidalia Sweet Onions	1	teaspoon garlic powder
		1	teaspoon seasoned salt
1	14½-ounce can tomatoes, chopped with juice		

Chop bacon into small pieces. Chop onion and cabbage into small wedges. Sauté bacon in deep skillet until almost crisp. Remove from pan with slotted spoon. Sauté onion in bacon grease until transparent, about 2 minutes. Add cabbage. Cook over medium heat until cabbage is still green but fork tender. Add tomatoes and juice, salt, sugar, garlic powder and seasoned salt. Continue to cook over medium heat until all ingredients are well blended. Add cooked bacon. Stir and serve. Serves 10 to 12.

" This dish waits on the stove well. You cannot use too many Vidalia sweet onions with the cabbage. It tastes great even if browns a little. "

Mrs. James E. Oller, Jr.
Mooleyville, KY

GREENS AND BEANS

1	large head, about 1 pound, escarole	2	cups chicken broth, canned or bouillon
1	large Vidalia Sweet Onion		Parmesan cheese, for serving
2	tablespoons butter or oleo	1	15-16 ounce can Cannellini beans, drained
			Salt and pepper, to taste

Rinse the escarole leaves several times. Discard wilted or discolored leaves. Slice onions thinly. In a large pot, sauté the onions in the butter until golden. Add the escarole leaves and sauté briefly, turning the onions and leaves frequently. Add chicken broth and simmer over low heat until the escarole is tender, about 20 to 30 minutes. Salt and pepper to taste. Add the Cannelline beans the last 5 minutes and heat thoroughly and serve with fresh, crusty bread. Sprinkle with Parmesan cheese. Serves 6.
Note: An old Italian recipe modernized.

Laura A. Zizzi
East Aurora, NY

GREEN BEANS PROVENCALE

1	pound fresh green beans, stemmed	4	large tomatoes, peeled, seeded and coarsely chopped
1	Vidalia Sweet Onion, coarsely chopped	½	cup dry white wine
4	cloves garlic, finely chopped	½	cup Nicoise or other imported black olives, pitted
2	tablespoons olive oil	1	tablespoons fresh lemon juice Coarsely ground black pepper

Find the thinnest, most tender green beans you can. Blanch the green beans in boiling water until just tender, about 3 to 4 minutes. Drain and refresh under cold water. The beans should still be a bit crispy. Reserve. In a deep skillet, cook the onion and garlic in olive oil over low heat for 5 minutes. Add the tomatoes and wine. Cook for 20 minutes longer, stirring occasionally. Toss the olives and reserved green beans into the skillet, heat thoroughly. Sprinkle with lemon juice and black pepper to taste. Serve immediately. Serves 6.

"This makes a magnificent side dish or light entree."

Eleanor Perry
New York, NY

GREEN BEANS WITH TOMATO SAUCE

4	strips regular bacon, un-cooked	1	16-ounce and one 8-ounce can cut green beans and juice
1	large Vidalia Sweet Onion	1	8-ounce can tomato sauce

Dice bacon slices and onion. Put bacon and onion into saucepan and brown, about 10 minutes, stirring often. Add beans with juice and stir in tomato sauce. Cover and simmer for 1 hour. Serves 6 to 8.

"A family favorite. Warm up leftovers in microwave. Also freezes well."

Linda Stewart
Wellington, KS

MOM'S GREEN BEAN DISH

3	packages frozen green beans	1	teaspoon instant chicken bouillon
2	8-ounce cans water chestnuts, sliced, drained	1	cup milk
1	jumbo Vidalia Sweet Onion, sliced and chopped	1	cup grated Cheddar cheese
		¼	cup chopped pimento
4	cups fresh mushrooms, halved and sliced	1	tablespoon sherry
		1	cup sliced almonds
4	tablespoons butter	1	tablespoon melted butter
2	tablespoons flour	¾	cup soft bread crumbs

Cook beans until barely tender. Drain. Drain water chestnuts. Combine with green beans and place in a greased flat 3-quart Pyrex dish. Sauté onions and mushrooms in butter. Add flour, bouillon and milk; cook slightly. Add cheese, pimento, and sherry. Cook a few minutes and pour over green beans and water chestnuts. Combine almonds, melted butter, and bread crumbs and place on top of green bean mixture. Bake in 350 degree oven for 35 to 45 minutes. Serves 12.

Mary Burney Shook
Raleigh, NC

NOODLE ONION KUGEL (PUDDING)

½	pound wide noodles	¼	cup vegetable oil
6	Vidalia Sweet Onions, cut up into large dices	3	eggs, beaten
		1	teaspoon salt

Cook noodles according to package directions. Drain. While noodles are cooking, sauté onions in oil until soft and just slightly brown. In large bowl, mix all ingredients together. Grease a 7x11-inch pan. Pour mixture into pan and bake uncovered at 350 degrees about 45 minutes until slightly brown on top. Serves 4 to 6.
Note: For a salt free diet, salt can be eliminated.

"Although I can purchase Vidalia Sweet Onions in the local supermarkets, my daughter sends me the Vidalia Sweet Onions from Bland Farms every year because they are so much better!"

Frances Jaffe
Rockville, MD

BRAISED ONIONS

6	to 8 tablespoons butter	½	teaspoon nutmeg
4	medium Vidalia Sweet Onions, sliced or diced	¾	cup Parmesan cheese
1	teaspoon salt		

Melt butter in heavy saucepan. Add onions, cover tightly, and cook over low heat 25 minutes or until tender. Add salt and nutmeg. Just before serving stir in cheese. Serves 8.

Jeane Cole
Pioneer, CA

CARAMELIZED VIDALIA ONIONS
OVER PASTA

4	to 5 medium, tennis ball size, Vidalia Sweet Onions, peeled and cut in chunks	1	10-ounce portion fresh cheese ravioli, or pasta of your choice
½	cup water		

Spray a non-stick skillet with an oil substitute and turn burner on high. Add onions, which will begin to sear immediately, and stir quickly until all sides are coated. Add ½ cup water and cover. Keep watching and stir every few minutes. After 10 minutes, turn heat down to medium, and add a little more water. For the next 30 minutes, check and stir periodically; you don't want them sticking to the pan. The secret to caramelizing is to cook them slowly. Then remove lid so liquid can cook down while you're boiling the pasta. These onions will reduce to about 1½ cups, and will be so sweet and buttery tasting. Serve onions over pasta. Serves 2.

Beverly McGuire
Hollywood, CA

CHEESE-SCALLOPED ONIONS

6 cups thinly sliced Vidalia
   Sweet Onion rings
¼ cup butter or margarine
¼ cup all-purpose flour

2 cups milk
½ teaspoon salt
2 cups shredded sharp Cheddar
   cheese, divided

Place onion rings in ungreased 1½-quart casserole. Melt butter in saucepan; blend in flour. Gradually stir in milk. Cook, stirring constantly until thick. Stir in salt and 1½ cups cheese. Pour over onions. Bake uncovered in moderate oven, 350 degrees, for 1 hour. Spread cheese over casserole last half hour. Serves 8.

Betty P. Staples
Ogunquit, ME

MABEL'S PAPRIKA ONIONS

4 tablespoons margarine
¼ cup honey
2 tablespoons water

1 tablespoon paprika
6 large Vidalia Sweet Onions,
   cut in half

Heat first 4 ingredients in small saucepan until margarine is melted. Place the onions, cut side up, in a lightly greased shallow casserole and drizzle with the heated sauce. Salt to taste, sparingly. Cover loosely with foil and bake 30 minutes at 350 degrees. Remove foil, baste with liquid from casserole and bake another 15 minutes. More paprika may be sprinkled over onions. Serves 6.
Note: Some onions are more moist than others so they may not need covering.

Doris W. Ranneberger
Bel Air, MD

ONION PARMESAN

2	to 4 Vidalia Sweet Onions		Garlic powder
1	14 1/2-16 ounce can chicken broth	½	cup Parmesan cheese, grated

Peel and half onions through center. Place in baking dish. Add chicken broth. Bake for ½ hour at 350 degrees, covered. Uncover onions. Sprinkle with garlic powder and Parmesan cheese. Continue baking until onions are tender and cheese is golden brown. Serves 4 to 8 depending on size of onions and size of appetites.
Note: Serve with meal as a delightful vegetable. Excellent with chicken, turkey, hamburgers, or pork.

Marie P. Hughes
Berlin, NH

SAUCY VIDALIAS ITALIANO

4	medium Vidalia Sweet Onions	1	8-ounce can spaghetti sauce
1	medium zucchini		Mozzarella cheese
2	tablespoons oil		

Cut onions and zucchini into slices and sauté in oil. Remove from heat and drain oil. Add spaghetti sauce. Top with Mozzarella cheese and bake uncovered in a 350 degree oven for 15 minutes.
Note: A great side dish or serve as main dish with salad and Italian bread.

Beverly A. Mussari
Cincinnati, OH

SIDE DISH VIDALIAS

Several large or medium-large
    Vidalia Sweet Onions
Butter

Salt and pepper
Steak sauce, Worcestershire sauce,
    BBQ sauce or soy sauce

Peel and quarter Vidalia Sweet Onions. Put in a casserole dish with a lid, or wrap in 2 layers of heavy duty foil. For each 2 onions, add ½ teaspoon salt, ¼ teaspoon pepper, 1½ tablespoons butter and 2 tablespoons of one of the sauces mentioned above. Cover, or seal with foil, and bake for 1 hour in 375 degree oven. Can also be put on BBQ grill for 1 to 1 ½ hours.
Note: For real onion lovers figure on 2 onions per serving other 1 onion per serving.

Noni Coleman
Knoxville, TN

SUSIE'S BLAND FARMS VIDALIA SWEET ONIONS AND POTATOES

4   Russet potatoes, sliced
4   Vidalia Sweet Onions, sliced
    Butter

Freshly ground pepper
Sour cream, light version ok

Place a piece of foil in a baking pan and layer sliced potatoes and sliced onions on top of foil. Top with pats of butter and generously grind pepper over top. Repeat layers until potatoes and onions are used up. Wrap foil around potatoes and onions. Bake in 350 degree oven for 1 hour. Serve and top with sour cream. Serves 4.
Note: Recipe may be increased or decreased as needed.

Susie Davis
Franktown, CO

SWEET VIDALIA ONIONS
AND MUSTARD GREENS

1	tablespoon olive oil	2	teaspoons fresh herbs
1	clove garlic, minced		Fresh lemon juice
½	Vidalia Sweet Onion, sliced		Red wine vinegar
1	cup mustard greens, washed well		Chili powder
½	medium tomato, seeded and diced		

Over medium heat, heat oil in sauté pan. Add garlic and stir 1 to 2 minutes. Add onions and greens and sauté 4 to 5 minutes. Stir in tomato and herbs. Cook 3 to 4 minutes longer, until greens are cooked and tomato heated through. Season to taste with lemon juice, vinegar, and a pinch of chili spice. Serves 1.
Note: Great as a side dish, or served over pasta or rice.

Robin C. Shoemaker
Brigantine, NJ

VEGGIE VIDALIA

Vidalia Sweet Onions, 1 per
serving

Worcestershire sauce

Peel onions. Scoop out root section to create small well. Place 6 drops Worcestershire sauce in each well. Place in microwave dish. Cover. Microwave on high 6 to 7 minutes for 2 onions. Adjust time upward when preparing large amounts. Serve as an accompanying side vegetable dish.

Mary F. Passano
Baltimore, MD

VIDALIAS A LA GORGONZOLA

1	bundle fresh asparagus tips, disregard stems	1	pint heavy cream
¼	cup olive oil	1	cup of Gorgonzola cheese, crumbled
1	cup Bland Farms Vidalia Sweet Onions		Salt
1	large clove of garlic, finely chopped		Pepper
		1	pound flat broad noodles

Poach asparagus tips. Cool and reserve. In olive oil, sauté onions and garlic until transparent. Add cream. As cream begins to heat, gradually add Gorgonzola, whisking until sauce becomes smooth. Add asparagus, salt, and pepper to taste. Cook pasta al dente. Mix together or serve asparagus mixture over pasta.

Joseph Guarino
Trenton, NJ

VIDALIA AND BACON VEGGIE

5	strips bacon	Seasoned salt
2	large Vidalia Sweet Onions	Pepper

Cut bacon into ½-inch pieces. Sauté until crisp. Remove all bacon fat. Dice 2 large Vidalia sweet onions and add to bacon in skillet. Add seasoned salt and pepper according to taste. Cover and simmer until onions are limp. Serves 3 to 4.
Note: Also good alone with crisp French Bread.

Ann M. Valuk
Rochester, NY

VIDALIA ONION AUGRATIN

2	pounds thinly sliced Vidalia Sweet Onions	¾	cup grated Parmesan cheese
2	tablespoons butter or margarine	¼	teaspoon white pepper
1½	cups herb flavored croutons	2	eggs
		1	cup milk
			Chives or slivered scallions

Sauté onions in butter in large non-stick frying pan, over medium heat until they are transparent but not brown. Sauté for about 20 to 30 minutes. Spread croutons over bottom of buttered 1½-quart gratin dish or shallow pan. Spread the sautéed onions over the croutons, then sprinkle on the cheese evenly. Lightly beat the pepper, eggs, and milk until blended and pour mixture over the onions. Cover tightly with plastic wrap and chill in refrigerator overnight or at least 6 hours for croutons to absorb the milk-egg mixture. Unwrap and bake in preheated 350 degree oven for 20 to 30 minutes or until knife inserted in center of dish comes out clean. Garnish with green scallions or chives. Serves 8 as a side dish.

"This gratin is a versatile side dish that works equally well with roasts, grilled meats or poultry. It is even great by itself for a luncheon dish."

James Mills
Denver, CO

VIDALIA ONION SHORTCAKE

1	Vidalia Sweet Onion	⅓	cup milk
¼	cup butter	1	small can creamed corn
1	cup sour cream	2	drops Tabasco sauce
1	box corn muffin mix (8 1/4 ounce)		Salt
		1	teaspoon dill
1	egg, beaten	1	cup grated sharp cheese

Sauté onions in butter. Let cool. Add sour cream to the mix. Blend egg with milk, creamed corn, Tabasco, salt and dill. Pour into a greased 8x8-inch pan. Sprinkle ½ cup cheese on top. Pat onion mixture on top then sprinkle with remaining cheese. Bake uncovered in 425 degree oven for 25 minutes. Serves 6 to 8.

Mary Win Immink
Suttons Bay, MI

VIDALIA ONIONS AND SWEET RED PEPPERS ISHMAEL

2	to 3 medium Vidalia Sweet Onions, sliced thin	3 to 4	tablespoons olive oil
1	large sweet red pepper	1	teaspoon fennel seeds
1	banana pepper, chopped	1	tablespoon fresh oregano
2	to 3 cloves garlic, mashed	1	tablespoon parsley
		½	cup white wine

Sauté onions, peppers and garlic in olive oil until just limp. Stir in fennel seeds and fresh herbs. Remove onion mixture and deglaze pan with white wine. Stir into sautéed vegetables and serve.

Note: Toss with cooked pasta, stir into cooked brown rice, spoon over hamburgers, serve with steak, fold into omelets, chill, use to top cold sandwiches.

Dody Parris
Easton, MD

BAKED POTATOES DELIGHT

4	to 6 red potatoes, par boiled until tender	2	cups coarsely chopped Vidalia Sweet Onions
1	stick butter	1½	cups grated Cheddar cheese
1	cup sour cream		Fresh ground pepper
			Salt, to taste

Grease a 9x13-inch baking dish. Preheat oven to 350 degrees. Layer cooked potatoes then butter, dot sour cream over butter, add onions and then cheese. Bake uncovered 20 to 25 minutes or until hot. Garnish with fresh ground pepper and salt. Serves 6 to 8.

Linda Wilson
Denison, TX

BAKED POTATOES SUPREME

2	large potatoes	4	pats butter
2	medium Vidalia Sweet Onions		Sour cream

Bake potatoes for approximately 1 hour. Chop Vidalia Sweet Onions. Scoop out potatoes and stir in butter and chopped onions. Put mixture back into shells. Bake again for 10 to 15 minutes. Remove and serve with sour cream.
Serves 2.

Mrs. Wm. J. Robinson
Hollywood, FL

DELICIOUS POTATOES

8	potatoes, cooked and diced		Pepper, to taste
1	cup chopped Baby Vidalia Sweet Onions	1	cup mayonnaise
½	pound sharp Cheddar cheese, grated	1	pound bacon, fried crisp & crumbled
	Salt, to taste	½	cup sliced green olives
			Cheddar cheese

Mix diced potatoes, onions, ½ pound Cheddar cheese, salt, pepper, and mayonnaise together. Top with bacon and olives and more Cheddar cheese.
Bake uncovered at 375 degrees for 30 minutes or until hot and bubbly. Serves 8.
Variation: Mix some of the cheese and bacon into the other ingredients as well as on top of the casserole.

Joan H. Inlow
Shelbyville, IA

NOT SO PLAIN POTATOES

2	cups water	1	big Vidalia Sweet Onion, sliced or diced
3	teaspoons bouillon powder		
1	tablespoon garlic powder	1	green pepper, sliced or diced
1	teaspoon salt	5	potatoes, cut and sliced
1	teaspoon pepper		

Put water in pan and add chicken bouillon powder, garlic powder, salt, pepper and heat until bouillon is dissolved. Add onion, green pepper, and potatoes. Boil until potato slices are well cooked. Serves 3 to 4.

Carol L. Martin
Detroit, MI

POTATO PUDDING

2	cups coarsely grated potato	2	tablespoons cream
1	cup minced Vidalia Sweet Onion		Salt, to taste
			Pepper, to taste
1	cup grated carrots	2	tablespoons butter

Combine first 3 ingredients together. Add cream, salt, and pepper. Place in buttered shallow casserole. Dot with butter. Cover and bake in 350 degree oven for 45 minute to 1 hour. Uncover near the end to brown top. Serves. 4.
Note: Great for 2 or a large group.

Paula M. Horr
Moorestown, NJ

SWEET ONION POTATOES

6	medium red potatoes		Salt, to taste
2	medium or 1 large Vidalia Sweet Onion, sliced or coarsely chopped		Pepper, to taste
		3	tablespoons margarine or butter
	Water to cover		

Boil potatoes and onions in water until done. Pour off water and mash cooked potatoes and onions together. Add salt, pepper and margarine or butter. Serve immediately or reheat in microwave before serving. Serves 4.

Grace-George Alexander-Greene
New York City, NY

SWEET ONION POTATO CAKES

6	baking potatoes, baked	2	eggs, beaten
2	large Vidalia Sweet Onions, minced		Sage, pinch
			Salt, to taste
4	inner celery stalks, minced		Pepper, to taste
1	red pepper, minced		

Scoop out the potatoes and discard the skins. Spray skillet with non-stick cooking spray. Combine the onions, celery, and pepper and sauté in skillet for 5 minutes. Mix potatoes and vegetables together. Add beaten eggs, then sage, salt, and pepper. Shape into patties and fry in butter until golden brown on both sides. Serves 10.

Dennis J. Drislane
Lynnfield, MA

VIDALIA SCALLOPED POTATOES

4	large potatoes	1½	teaspoons salt
2	Vidalia Sweet Onions	½	teaspoon pepper
1½	cups half and half	3	tablespoons butter
2	tablespoons all-purpose flour		

Peel and slice potatoes in ¼-inch slices. Peel and slice onions in ¼-inch slices. Layer potatoes and onions in lightly greased casserole dish. Mix half and half, flour, salt, and pepper until flour is dissolved. Pour over potatoes and onions and then dot with butter. Bake uncovered at 350 degrees for 1 hour, gently stirring occasionally to thicken. Serves 4.

Elba P. Wongus
Vienna, VA

SPANISH RICE

1¼	cups rice, uncooked	1	green pepper, diced
1	14½-ounce can tomatoes with spices	2	large Vidalia Sweet Onions, chopped
1	8-ounce can tomato sauce	3	tablespoons chopped celery
Salt and pepper, to taste		Vegetable oil or non-stick cooking spray	

Mix first 3 ingredients together and add salt and pepper to taste. Saute pepper, onions and celery in a little vegetable oil or cooking spray and mix with first 3 ingredients. Pour into lightly greased casserole dish and dot with butter or margarine. Bake covered slowly in 275 degree oven for 1 to 1½ hours. Serves 8.

Sophie Klene
Arlington Heights, IL

CREAMED CHUNKY SPINACH

*A THICK, RICH, CREAMED SPINACH ENHANCED BY CHUNKS OF
VIDALIA SWEET ONIONS AND WORCESTERSHIRE SAUCE*

2	boxes frozen chopped spinach	4	tablespoons flour
1	large Vidalia Sweet Onion	3	slices white bread
¼	pound butter	¼	teaspoon nutmeg
1	tablespoon bacon drippings		Salt, to taste
			Pepper, to taste
			Worcestershire sauce, to taste

Cook spinach and drain well. Chop onion (chunky) and sauté in butter. Add bacon drippings when onion is sautéed. Stir in flour to make roux, until thick. Wet bread with water and squeeze dry. Break up bread into small bits and add to spinach. Add spinach mixture to roux and mix well. Add nutmeg, salt, pepper, and Worcestershire sauce. Serves 4 to 6.

*Edward R. Schultheis
Massapequa, NY*

SUMMER SQUASH PARMESAN

3	cups thinly sliced summer squash	½	to 1 cup water
1	cup thinly sliced Vidalia Sweet Onion	½	cup Parmesan cheese

Place squash and onions and water in microwave safe dish and cover tightly with plastic wrap. Cook for 10 minutes on HIGH until done. Drain; add cheese. Microwave 3 minutes more. Serves 4.

*Mary Burney Shook
Raleigh, NC*

TWICE-BAKED SQUASH BOATS

3	acorn or butternut squash	1	tablespoon lemon pepper
1	stick butter or margarine		Salt, to taste, optional
2	jumbo or 3 medium Vidalia Sweet Onions, chopped	1	cup Italian seasoned bread crumbs
1	tablespoon garlic powder		

Halve squash lengthwise and scoop out seeds and stringy pulp. Place cut side down on shallow pan or cookie sheet lined with aluminum foil. Crimp up sides of foil so juices are contained. Bake 30 to 45 minutes or until done at 350 degrees. Remove from oven; place pan on rack to cool. After a few minutes, turn squash right side up. While squash is cooling, melt butter in large skillet and sauté onions until very brown. Scoop squash from shells and add directly into skillet, mashing with fork; remove from heat. Stir in garlic powder, lemon pepper, and salt. Refill the 6 squash shells with contents of skillet, leaving ¼-inch at top. Sprinkle with bread crumbs. Dot with more butter, if desired. Return to oven and bake 20 minute at 350 degrees using same foil lined pan. Serves 6.

Note: In place of lemon pepper a combination of 1 teaspoon pepper, 1 tablespoon grated lemon rind, 3 tablespoons lemon juice including pulp may be used. This recipe can be prepared up to 24 hours ahead and refrigerated without bread crumbs. Add these just before baking.

Melinda Boyer
Atlanta, GA

GREEN VEGETABLE PIE

2	cups broccoli	3	eggs
½	cups chopped Vidalia Sweet Onion	1	cup prepared biscuit mix
½	cup chopped green pepper	¼	teaspoon pepper
1½	cups milk	2	cups shredded cheese

Boil broccoli 5 minutes. Drain and mix with onion, and green pepper. Place in lightly buttered quiche dish. Combine milk, eggs, prepared biscuit mix, and pepper and mix well. Pour over vegetables and bake uncovered in 400 degree oven for 35 minutes or until brown.

Phyllis A. Lucas
Brookhaven, PA

STEAMED FRESH VEGETABLE MIX

2	Vidalia Sweet Onions	8	to 10 pods fresh okra
1	bunch fresh broccoli	4	peeled carrots
5	red new potatoes	½	cup water or chicken broth
½	head cauliflower		Salt and pepper, to taste

Cut vegetables into bite sized pieces, except for okra, leave whole. Place in microwave safe dish with cover. Add water or chicken broth and microwave on HIGH for 15 minutes or until carrots pierce easily with fork. Salt and pepper to taste. If using water, 2 tablespoons of margarine added after cooking tastes great. Stir every 5 minutes during cooking. Serves 8 to 10.

Sherry Summers
Pasadena, TX

VEGETABLE CASSEROLE

	French style green beans		Salt, to taste
1	small bag frozen corn		Pepper, to taste
1	cup Vidalia Sweet Onions	1½	stack round butter flavored
1	cup mild Cheddar cheese		crackers, crushed
1	8-ounce carton sour cream	1	stick margarine, melted
1	10¾-ounce can cream of mushroom soup, undiluted		

Combine all ingredients together except ¾ cup crushed crackers and margarine. Pour mixture into buttered casserole dish and top with crushed crackers. Drizzle melted butter over top of crackers. Bake uncovered at 350 degrees for 30 minutes.

Patricia Raynolds
Woodstock, VT

VEGETARIAN INDIAN CORN & RICE

2 tablespoons oil
1 teaspoon margarine or butter
1 large Vidalia Sweet Onion, chopped
1 15-ounce can unsalted corn, drained
2½ teaspoons cumin
1½ teaspoons celery salt
2 teaspoons salad herbs and/or parsley
1 to 2 tablespoons soy sauce
1½ cups cooked brown rice, preferably long grain
1 teaspoon sour cream or margarine

Heat oil and margarine on medium heat in large skillet. Add chopped onion, corn and all seasonings. Sauté on medium heat until onions are soft. Add brown rice and sauté about another 5 to 10 minutes on medium heat. Dollop with an additional teaspoon margarine and/or sour cream and you're ready to eat. Serves 4.

Theresa A. Gonzales
Tampa, FL

CHICKEN AND VEGETABLE STIR-FRY

4 boneless, skinless chicken breast halves
1 pound fresh broccoli
2 tablespoons vegetable oil
2 tablespoons water
1 large Vidalia Sweet Onion, chunked
2 medium-size red bell peppers, chunked
½ pound fresh mushrooms, quartered
⅓ cup low-sodium teriyaki sauce
¼ teaspoon crushed red pepper
1 cup rice, cooked according to package directions

Cut chicken into 1-inch squares. Cut broccoli flowerets into bite-sized pieces. Peel the stalk and cut into thin slices. Heat oil in large skillet over high heat. Add chicken and stir-fry 1 minute. Add 2 tablespoons water; cover and cook 2 minutes, stirring once. Add broccoli and onions, bell peppers and mushrooms; stir-fry 3 minutes. Add teriyaki sauce and crushed red pepper. Cook, stirring until ingredients are covered with sauce. Serve over hot rice. Serves 4 to 6.

Mary C. Zelensky
Burlington, NJ

STIR~FRY LIVER AND ONIONS

Vidalia Sweet Onions
All-purpose flour
Cornstarch
Liver, any variety beef, calf's
    or fresh lamb, sliced ½-
    inch thick and each slice
    made into ½-inch strips

Bacon fat
Chicken or beef broth
Salt
Pepper

Peel and quarter Vidalia Sweet Onions. Separate wedges into cups. Mix flour and cornstarch, equal amounts of each. Dredge liver strips and shake off excess. In large heavy fry pan or wok, heat bacon fat to hot. Stir-fry onions till tender crisp. Remove and save. Stir-fry liver, handful at a time, until almost done. Set aside. Cook all liver. Return liver and onions and seasonings to pan to get hot. Pour broth over and stir as it makes gravy. Ladle over cooked rice, potatoes or noodles.

Ann M.C. Kittredge
Tremonton, UT

SWEET VIDALIA STIR~FRY

1 pound turkey kielbasa, sliced in ½-inch rounds
4 to 5 tablespoons margarine, divided

1 jumbo Vidalia Sweet Onion, sliced lengthwise in eighths or sixteenths
1 16-ounce bag, or less, frozen sugar snap peas
Soy or other bottled stir-fry sauce

In large skillet or wok, sauté kielbasa slices in 1 tablespoon margarine over medium high heat until browned. Push to one side of skillet. Add remaining margarine and sauté onion until almost tender. Mix the two together in skillet, then fold in the sugar snap peas and sprinkle with soy sauce, if desired. Simmer uncovered over medium heat until peas are tender but not overcooked. Can be served alone or with rice. Serves 4 to 5.

"This is a quick and easy meal to prepare. Ingredient amounts are not critical and recipe can be easily halved."

Karen Sliva
Tewksbury, MA

Meat, Chicken & Seafood

BARBECUED HAMBURGERS

1	pound of ground beef	¼	cup vinegar
2	tablespoons fat or salad oil	1	tablespoon granulated sugar
1½	cups catsup	½	teaspoon dry mustard
1	large or medium Vidalia Sweet Onion, sliced		

Shape ground beef into 4 large patties, add fat or oil to skillet and brown patties. Combine catsup, onion, vinegar, sugar and dry mustard. Pour over patties. Cover, simmer 20 minutes. Place on buns or bread or eat as is. Serves 4.

Charmaine Leavitt
Kalamazoo, MI

BURGER STUFFED VIDALIAS

6	large Vidalia Sweet Onions	1	teaspoon chili powder
2	tablespoons vegetable oil	½	teaspoon salt
1	pound lean ground beef	⅛	teaspoon pepper
2	tablespoons chopped bell pepper	3	slices American cheese
2	tablespoons dry bread crumbs	1	8-ounce can tomato sauce

Peel onions and cook in boiling salted water until tender. Drain and cool. Slice off top ⅓ of each onion. Scoop out centers to make cups. Chop ½ cup of centers and sauté in oil along with beef and peppers for 5 minutes. Mix in crumbs, chili powder, salt, and pepper. Fill onion cups with mixture and place in a shallow baking dish. Top each with ½ slice of the cheese cut into a triangular shape. Pour the tomato sauce on top and bake at 350 degrees for 30 minutes, occasionally basting onions with sauce. If desired, a small amount of tomato sauce can be put on top of the meat before adding cheese and then the remainder of tomato sauce on top of cheese. Serves 6.

"This is an old recipe and everyone I have given it to through the years LOVES it. It is very good!"

Joan Jones
Marshall, TX

VIDALIA SWEET ONION CHILE CON CARNE

2	pounds ground beef	¼	teaspoon crushed red pepper flakes
1	tablespoon cumin		
⅛	teaspoon cinnamon	1	15-ounce can kidney beans, rinsed and drained
1	large Vidalia Sweet Onion, large dice		
		1	15-ounce can tomato sauce
3	medium cloves garlic, medium diced	1	8-ounce can whole tomatoes with juice, and quartered
¼	teaspoon freshly ground pepper	6	ounces your favorite beer

In Dutch oven, sauté the ground beef until browned. Drain, add remaining ingredients and cover with lid slightly ajar. Simmer 2 hours. Refrigerate overnight, reheat and serve for lunch or dinner. Garnish with raw chopped Vidalia sweet onion, pickled jalapeño slices (or finely diced fresh jalapeño), and shredded Cheddar cheese.

Laurie B. Longfield
Aspen, CO

CHINESE BEEF WITH VIDALIA SWEET ONIONS

1	pound beef tenderloin	½	teaspoon baking soda
3	tablespoons dry sherry	¼	teaspoon salt
1½	tablespoons soy sauce	1	clove garlic, crushed
2	teaspoons oyster sauce	1½	tablespoons vegetable oil
1	teaspoon sugar	3	medium Vidalia Sweet Onions, thinly sliced
1	teaspoon cornstarch		

Remove and discard fat from meat; cut meat across the grain into thin slices. Combine next 8 ingredients, mix well and add beef. Cover and refrigerate at least 3 hours. Heat oil in wok or skillet over high heat. Stir fry onions in oil, until golden about 3 to 5 minutes. Transfer onions to serving plate and keep warm. Add about ⅓ of the meat to wok, spreading out slices so they do not overlap. Cook slices on each side until lightly browned, about 2 to 3 minutes. Remove meat from wok and arrange over onions. Repeat twice to cook remaining meat. Serves 4.

Eleanor J. Byer
Pittsburgh, PA

PENNSYLVANIA DUTCH BEEF ONION STEW

2	pounds beef cubes	1	7-ounce jar olives, drained
2	14 1/2-16 ounce cans tomatoes	2	large Vidalia Sweet Onions
¾	cup chopped green pepper		Olive oil
		1	cup brown rice, raw

Mix beef, tomatoes, green pepper and olives together in stew kettle. Fry onions in skillet with olive oil until brown. Add to stew and let simmer for 4½ to 5 hours or until tender. One hour prior to serving, add brown rice and stir gently.
Serves 6 to 8.

"You don't need a recipe–your onions are so sweet, we can eat them raw!"

Cindy Berger
Chester Springs, PA

SHERRIED BEEF-ONION BAKE

2	tablespoons margarine	¼	teaspoon kitchen bouquet
2	tablespoons flour	2	to 3 large Vidalia Sweet
	Pepper		Onions, cut in wedges
1	cup water	¾	cup croutons
¼	cup sherry	⅓	cup shredded Swiss cheese
2	tablespoons beef bouillon granules	2	tablespoons grated Parmesan cheese
1	pound stew beef, cut into bite sized pieces		Parsley flakes

In medium saucepan, melt margarine. Stir in flour and pepper. Add water, sherry, and bouillon granules. Cook and stir until thickened and bubbly. Cook and stir 1 minute more. Remove from heat. Stir in beef and kitchen bouquet. Place onion wedges in 1½-quart casserole. Spoon meat mixture on top. Cover casserole and bake in 375 degree oven for 1¾ to 2 hours, until meat is tender. Arrange croutons on top. Sprinkle with Swiss cheese, Parmesan and parsley. Return to oven. Bake uncovered 5 minutes more. Serves 4.
Note: If desired, the croutons and cheeses can be omitted.

Betty Atkins
Birmingham, MI

STEAK VIDALIA

2   tablespoons butter, divided
2   Vidalia Sweet Onions, sliced   1   can beef broth
4   serving slices roast beef,   4   slices mild Cheddar cheese
     thick

Melt ½ the butter in a casserole dish. Layer Vidalia sweet onion slices over melted butter. Repeat with roast beef. Pour beef broth over this. Cover with slices of cheese. Dot with balance of butter. Bake at 350 degrees covered for ½ hour. Any liquid remaining in casserole may be thickened to use as gravy or use as is over servings.

Ada Z. Gregary
Prescott, AZ

TEX-MEX STEAK AND ONIONS

⅓   cup Worcestershire sauce   3   limes
¼   cup white wine vinegar   2   large Vidalia Sweet Onions
1   tablespoon oil   Flour tortillas
3   to 4 crushed garlic cloves   Extra Worcestershire sauce
     Salt and pepper
2   pounds round steak, cubed
     once

In a small bowl, mix first 6 ingredients, add juice and rinds of 2 limes saving rinds. Cut onions in half and slice into long thing strips. Soak meat and onions in marinade with lime rinds for 1 hour or more, turning occasionally if possible. Drain off marinade and throw away with lime rinds. Put onions in foil or in a tin pie plate. Cook meat and onions on hot grill. While meat is cooking sprinkle with extra Worcestershire sauce and lime juice. Keep onions stirred so they won't burn. Cook until meat is done and the onions are fairly dry. If cooked in an oven, use a pan with a rack and set the oven to 35 degrees and cook for 30 to 45 minutes. Slice meat into long thin strips depending on size of flour tortillas used. Make small party size tortillas by cutting out small circles from large flour tortillas. Heat tortillas right before serving. Fill tortillas with meat and onions, then top with any of the following, Vidalia guacamole, (recipe page 132), salsa, sour cream, or shredded cheese.

Rhonda Hitch
Kathleen, GA

VIDALIA GUACAMOLE

1	tomato, chopped fine		Juice of ½ lime
2	ripe avocados, mashed	1	tablespoons vegetable oil
½	cup Vidalia Sweet Onions, minced	2	to 3 tablespoons vegetable juice
1	small clove garlic, minced		Salt
1	or 2 jalapeño peppers, minced		Pepper

In food blender or by hand, mix all ingredients together. Put in a small bowl, cover and chill at least 1 hour before serving. Serve with Tex-Mex Steak and Onions, page 131.

Rhonda Hitch
Kathleen, GA
Sixth Place Winner
Georgia National Fair

CHICKEN AND ONIONS

4	Vidalia Sweet Onions	Salt and pepper
½	cup vegetable oil	Paprika
	Garlic powder	Fresh parsley, chopped
3	pounds boneless chicken breasts	

Peel and slice onions ¼-inch thick. Heat oil in a heavy pan. Sauté onion slices on one side until lightly browned. Sprinkle with garlic powder. Turn the onions and put chicken on top. Season the chicken with salt, pepper, garlic powder and paprika, to taste. Cover pan. Reduce heat to low and slowly cook for 30 minutes. Turn the chicken so the onions are on top and add more paprika. Cook 30 more minutes or until chicken is tender. Sprinkle parsley on top. Serves 5 to 6.

Linda Fishman
Christiana, PA

CHICKEN POCKETS WITH VIDALIA YOGURT SAUCE

4	boneless, skinless chicken breasts	1	tablespoon margarine or oil
	Bottled Italian dressing or your favorite marinade	1	cup plain yogurt
1	to 2 Vidalia Sweet Onions, thinly sliced	4	pita bread pockets

Marinate chicken breasts in Italian dressing for 3 to 4 hours or overnight. Grill chicken about 10 to 12 minutes over charcoal or on gas grill. Do not overcook. While chicken is grilling, prepare sauce by sautéing onions in oil until lightly browned. Remove from heat and stir in yogurt. If necessary, warm gently. To serve, cut end from pita pocket, insert chicken breast and fill with yogurt sauce. Serves 4.
Note: Use as a substitute for hamburgers on a summer evening cookout.

Barbara Hevberger
Wilmington, DE

CHICKEN SKILLET STEW

1	pound fresh ground chicken	1	10 3/4-ounce can tomato soup
1	large Vidalia Sweet Onion		
3	medium potatoes	1	7-ounce can kernel corn, drained
3	large carrots		
1 to 2 tablespoons water		1	16-ounce can stewed tomatoes, undrained
3	stalks celery		
1	green pepper		Salt and Pepper
			Oregano

In your largest skillet (an electric skillet works excellently), brown ground chicken and sliced onion. Peel potatoes and carrots and cut into chunks. Layer on top of ground chicken. Add 1 to 2 tablespoons water and steam over medium heat while preparing other vegetables. Add remaining ingredients and bring to a boil. Reduce heat and simmer covered until potatoes are done. While stew is simmering, add salt, pepper and oregano to taste. Stir occasionally to loosen from bottom of skillet. Serves 6.

Louise M. Lowande
North Plainfield, NJ

CURRIED CHICKEN

1	chicken, cut into parts or pieces	½	clove garlic, pressed or ¼ teaspoon garlic powder
	Oil or margarine for browning	½	teaspoon cayenne pepper, medium hot
4	large Vidalia Sweet Onions, cut into ⅛'s		Salt
1	to 2 tablespoons curry powder (madras preferred)		Pepper

Place chicken in large heavy sauce pot or roaster and brown on high for 5 to 10 minutes, turning chicken occasionally. Reduce heat to medium. Add Vidalia sweet onions. Add all the seasonings, stir and cook for 30 to 40 minutes longer, stirring occasionally. Serves 4 to 6. Serve over your favorite rice.

"This recipe was created especially for my family to enjoy Vidalia Sweet Onion and ONLY VIDALIA SWEET ONIONS CAN BE USED IN THIS RECIPE!"

Joyce DiBenedetto-Colton
Miami, FL

GOURMET CHICKEN LIVER SAUTÉ-OLE

2	Vidalia Sweet Onions, chopped		Salt, to taste
			Pepper, to taste
3	tablespoons oil	2	tablespoons paprika
1	pound chicken livers	2	tablespoons red wine
8	ounces sliced mushrooms	1	cup chopped fresh cilantro
1	teaspoon granulated garlic or 4 cloves fresh garlic, crushed, or ½ teaspoon garlic powder		

Sauté chopped Vidalia sweet onions in oil until lightly browned. Season with garlic, salt, and pepper to taste. Add 1 tablespoon paprika and mix well. Add chicken livers and sauté until well done, about 10 minutes. Add remaining paprika and red wine. Continue cooking 5 minutes, stirring. Sprinkle with cilantro and serve over brown rice. Serves 3 to 4.

Susan Klein
Secaucers, NJ

HAWAIIAN CHICKEN

1	20-ounce can pineapple, sliced	½	cup pineapple or peach preserves
3	whole chicken breasts, split	1	tablespoon soy sauce
1½	teaspoons salt	1	tablespoon white vinegar
3	tablespoons vegetable oil or margarine		
1	large Vidalia Sweet Onion, sliced		
1	green pepper, sliced		

Drain pineapple. Sprinkle chicken with salt and brown in margarine. Cover and cook until chicken is done. Remove chicken and add onions and green peppers to skillet. Cook 1 to 2 minutes. Return chicken to skillet. Combine preserves, soy sauce, and vinegar and pour over chicken. Cook about 3 minutes, turning chicken to glaze. Remove chicken to platter and add pineapple to sauce, heat thoroughly and spoon over chicken. Serves 6.

A Friend

SERGIO'S WHITE CHICKEN

1	cup all-purpose flour	1	stick butter
1	teaspoon tarragon	½	pound mushrooms, chopped
	Salt	1	tablespoon cognac
	Pepper	1	cup milk
1½	pound chicken breasts, cut into small pieces	1	pound Vidalia sweet onions, chopped

In a bag, mix flour, tarragon, salt, pepper, and pieces of chicken. When chicken is well coated with the mixture of flour, sauté it slowly in a pan containing ½ the stick of butter. When the pieces are golden, add mushrooms, then cognac and milk and cook a bit longer. Set aside. In a large pan, combine the remaining butter and onions and sauté very lightly until onions are barely wilted. Pour the chicken in the center of a serving platter and place onions around it. Serves 4.
Note: Serve with rice or buttered noodles.

Sergio Cervetti
Brooklyn, NY

SPECIAL CHICKEN AND ONIONS

4	chicken breasts	1	Vidalia Sweet Onion, sliced
3	tablespoons all-purpose flour	½	cup water
¼	teaspoon basil	¼	cup white vermouth, optional
¼	teaspoon oregano		Freshly ground pepper
2	tablespoons olive oil		Salt, to taste

Dredge chicken in mixture of flour, basil and oregano. Brown chicken in oil in skillet, uncovered. Add onion, water, wine, pepper and salt. Cover and gently simmer 45 minutes or until done. Serves 4.
Note: Serve over rice.

Ann Kelk
Jamestown, NC

LAMB STUFFED VIDALIAS

4	large Vidalia Sweet Onions or 1 for each person	2	tablespoons Worcestershire sauce
1	pound ground lamb	¼	cup quick cooking oats
1	medium carrot, grated	1	large egg

Core onions removing all but the 2 outer layers. Chop and freeze the inside layers for another use. Combine all remaining ingredients and stuff into the Vidalia sweet onions. Wrap them in foil and bake at 350 degrees for 40 minutes or until onions are tender. Serves 4.
Note: Sausage or veal may be substituted for lamb.

Paul Atkinson
Indianapolis, IN

LIVER ONION DELIGHT

6	slices smoky maple bacon	2	large Vidalia Sweet Onions
1	pound fresh calves liver, ½-inch slices	½	teaspoon salt
½	cup all-purpose flour	½	teaspoon black pepper
		4	tablespoons French dressing

Slow fry bacon until crisp. Dredge liver in seasoned flour. Remove bacon from frying pan, place onions in 2 tablespoons bacon drippings. Smother onions until wilted. Remove from frying pan and add 2 more tablespoons bacon drippings. Add liver and brown lightly over low heat about 10 minutes. Pour French dressing over liver and add onions. Smother 10 minutes. Sprinkle bacon on top and serve. Serves 4.

Eugenia English
Dallas, TX

LIVER AND VIDALIA ONIONS

3	medium Vidalia Sweet Onions, thinly sliced	4	teaspoons pepper
6	tablespoons vegetable shortening, divided	2	cups all-purpose flour
		1	pound liver
4	teaspoons salt	½	cup white wine
		1	cup sour cream

Sauté onions in 3 tablespoons vegetable shortening. Add 2 teaspoons salt and 2 teaspoons pepper to flour. Dredge liver with flour until well coated. Brown in 3 tablespoons vegetable shortening until brown. Add onions and wine. Reduce heat and simmer until liver is nearly dry, about 15 minutes. Add sour cream and reheat until hot. Serves 6.
Note: Serve with your favorite rice.

"So now even the kids eat liver!"

Mrs. E. R. Edwards
Ft. Worth, TX

PORK CHOP WITH PINEAPPLE

1	pork chop	1	Vidalia Sweet Onion
1	8-ounce can crushed pineapple	1	orange, optional
	Vegetables, any left over or any small amounts of fresh		

Dice or cube all ingredients. Cook pork in non-stick wok or pan using no oil. Cook until browned. Add all other ingredients and cook until onion is clear and meat cooked through. Serves 2.
Note: Serve over rice or pasta or can be eaten alone.

Lynn Smith
San Diego, CA

BAKED PORK CHOPS WITH VIDALIAS

6	center cut pork chops, 1-inch	⅓	can water, milk or thick cream
6	¼-inch slices Vidalia Sweet Onion	1	10¾-ounce can tomato soup, undiluted

Preheat oven to 375 or 400 degrees. Place pork chops in lightly greased baking pan and place 1 slice Vidalia sweet onion on each chop. Mix liquid with tomato soup and pour over pork chops. Bake uncovered for 1 hour. Serves 6.

"I'm all for Vidalias!"

Violette B. Evensen
Pepperell, MA

KIT'S ROAST PORK FOR ONION LOVERS

¼	cup margarine or butter	1	teaspoon basil
1	carrot, diced	1	teaspoon parsley
1	green or yellow pepper, diced		Pepper, to taste
		1	cup chopped mushrooms
1	cup diced celery	2	Vidalia Sweet Onions, 1 sliced and 1 diced
1	cup apple juice or water		
⅛	teaspoon sage	1	8-ounce package cornbread crumbs
⅛	teaspoon thyme		
⅛	teaspoon garlic		Loin of pork

In saucepan, melt butter or margarine, add carrot, pepper, celery, apple juice, herbs and diced onion. Cook carefully until soft. Add more liquid if needed. Add breadcrumbs and toss lightly. Take roast, slice ¾ way down, put crumb mixture between each slice, then insert a slice of onion next to mixture and meat. Take remaining onion slices and place around meat in roasting pan. Roast 1½ hours in 350 degree oven.

Kathleen H. Cole
Boonton Township, NJ

VIDALIA ONION SALSA WITH PORK TENDERLOIN STRIPS

2	cups Vidalia Sweet Onions, diced	3	tablespoons sugar
		½	teaspoon sweet hot mustard
1	cup fresh tomatoes, diced	¼	cup bell pepper, diced
1	8-ounce can tomato sauce	1	teaspoon pickling spice wrapped in a small cloth bag
½	cup white vinegar		
	Dash of salt		Boneless pork tenderloin
	Dash of Accent		

To make salsa, combine all ingredients except pork in a saucepan. Bring to a good bubbling boil. Reduce heat and simmer for about 30 minutes. Remove pickling spice bag and serve with pork tenderloin strips. To prepare pork tenderloin strips, slice boneless pork tenderloin into 1-inch strips. Sauté in saucepan with butter until tender and done. Use toothpicks to serve.

George DeFore
Byron, GA
Fourth Place Winner
Georgia National Fair

VISALIA (VIDALIA) CASSEROLE

4   to 6 chops, lamb chops or veal chops
1   to 2 Vidalia Sweet Onions, sliced
1   green pepper, sliced
1   cup rice, brown, white or wild, raw
1   16-ounce can cut tomatoes, undrained

Place chops in casserole. Slice onions, and peppers and place on top of meat. Put 1 cup rice around chops and put tomatoes on top. Season with salt and pepper, parsley or basil. Cover and cook in 325 to 350 degree oven for 1 hour. Serves 4 to 6.

Margaret Kloster
Visalia, CA

SAUSAGE DRESSING

3   ribs of celery, chopped
1   Vidalia Sweet Onion, chopped
1   bell pepper, chopped
1   clove garlic, chopped
1   stick margarine
1   pound bulk hot sausage
1   4-ounce can mushrooms, drained
½   skillet cornbread
1   cup cream or milk
1   cup chicken broth
3   eggs, beaten
Salt and pepper, to taste

Sauté celery, onion, bell pepper and garlic in butter with pork sausage. Add mushrooms, cornbread, milk, broth and slightly beaten eggs. Mix well. Put into casserole dish and bake uncovered at 350 degrees for 45 minutes.

Don Adams
Zachary, LA

CURRIED SHRIMP

1   tablespoon olive oil
1   tablespoon unsalted butter
½   clove garlic, pressed or
        ¼ teaspoon garlic powder
1   pound raw fresh shrimp,
        peeled and deveined

4   Vidalia Sweet Onions, cut
        into eighths
2   tablespoons curry
        powder (madras preferred)
¼   teaspoon cayenne pepper
     Salt and pepper
1   to 2 cups water

Heat large skillet to medium heat and add olive oil, butter, and garlic. When butter melts, add shrimp and reduce heat to low. Cook shrimp on one side about 2 minutes. Then turn to cook on the other side for 1 minute. Transfer shrimp to a bowl, leaving juices in skillet. Add Vidalia sweet onions and seasonings. Stir and add water. Adjust salt. Stir, cover and simmer onions for 20 to 30 minutes on low. Stir in the shrimp and cook uncovered for 3 minutes. Taste for seasoning. Serves 2 to 4.
Note: Serve with your favorite rice.

Joyce DiBeneddeto-Colton
Miami, FL

ONION AND SHRIMP CREOLE

4   strips bacon
3   Vidalia Sweet Onions,
        chopped into large pieces
1   green pepper, chopped into
        large pieces

1   pound raw cleaned shrimp
1   8-ounce can tomato sauce

Fry bacon in large pan. Remove bacon from pan. In bacon grease, fry onions and green pepper until limp. Add raw, cleaned shrimp and tomato sauce and mix together. Cover for 6 minutes and stir. Serve on white rice. Crumble bacon on top. Serves 4.

Mali E. Spaeth
Flushing, NY

PAN FRIED ORANGE ROUGHY

4   fresh orange roughy fillets
¼   cup all-purpose flour
     Salt
     Pepper

1   tablespoons margarine or
     butter
1   large Vidalia Sweet Onion
     Parsley for garnish

Rinse fillets and pat dry. Coat with flour mixed with salt and pepper. Heat butter in skillet on medium heat. Add chopped onion and gently cook 3 to 5 minutes. Add fillets to pan and fry each side for 2 minutes turning each fillet over completely twice. Total cooking time is about 8 to 10 minutes according to thickness of fillets. Garnish with parsley. Serves 4.

Nancy J. Lentz
Findlay, OH

SCRAMBLED EGGS WITH ONIONS AND SMOKED SALMON

2   to 3 tablespoons cooking oil
1   large Vidalia Sweet Onion
4   eggs

4   slices smoked salmon
     Salt
     Pepper

Chop onion and sauté in oil over low heat being careful not to burn. Beat eggs in dish. Cut salmon into bite sized pieces and add to eggs. Add egg and salmon mixture to onions and stir until eggs are firm and salmon changes color. Salt and pepper to taste. Serves 2.
Note: Serve with a toasted bagel.

Joseph Gordaon
New York, NY

TUNA STUFFED ONIONS

2	large Vidalia Sweet Onions	¼	teaspoon paprika
1	6 1/8-ounce can low fat, low salt tuna in water	2	tablespoons salad dressing or mayonnaise
½	celery stick, diced	¼	teaspoon black pepper

Remove skin and top from onions. Cut ¾ down from top. Spoon out most of remaining onion and chop fine. Drain and mix tuna in a bowl. Add onions, celery, paprika, and salad dressing. Put mixture back in onion shells. Sprinkle black pepper and paprika over the top and serve. Serves 2 to 4.

Robert Vitagliano
Niagara Falls, NY

VIDALIA ONION AND TUNA

1	large or medium Vidalia Sweet Onion	1	6 1/8-ounce can light chunky style tuna, drained

Slice onion into thin slices. Break up chunks of tuna onto a plate and place onion slices over tuna, covering completely. Cover with plastic wrap and refrigerate for at least 1 hour so the onion can permeate through the tuna. Serves 2 to 3.
Note: Serve with creamed peas or macaroni and cheese.

Mrs. George W. McMahon
Shadyside, OH

Pies, Quiche & Omelets

ALBERT'S VIDALIA SWEET ONION PIE

1	9-inch pastry shell, unbaked	1	cup sour cream
2	pounds Vidalia Sweet Onions, thinly sliced	¼	teaspoon salt
		½	teaspoon white pepper
1	stick butter or margarine	¼	teaspoon Tabasco sauce
3	eggs, well beaten		Grated Parmesan cheese

Sauté onions in butter, stirring frequently to avoid burning. Combine eggs and sour cream. Stir together the sautéed onions and egg mixture. Season with salt, pepper, and Tabasco. Pour into prepared pie shell and top with Parmesan cheese. Bake at 450 degrees 20 minutes then reduce heat to 325 degrees and bake another 10 minutes or until filling is set. Serves 6.

Albert J. Reber
Lakeville, MN

Variation: Use 2 9-inch pastry shells and bake at 350 degrees for 8 minutes. Follow recipe above pour into pie shells and bake at 350 degrees for 20 minutes then reduce heat to 325 degrees and continue baking for 15 minutes or until top of pie is slightly brown. Yield 2 pies.

Joan Casson Sauer
Locust Valley, NY

CAROLYN'S VIDALIA SWEET ONION PIE

1	cup cracker crumbs	2	eggs
5	tablespoons melted butter	¾	cup half and half
2½	cups thinly sliced Vidalia Sweet Onions		Salt
			Pepper
2	tablespoons olive oil	½	cup grated Swiss cheese

Combine crumbs and butter. Press into an 8-inch deep dish pie pan. Bake 8 minutes at 350 degrees. Sauté onions in olive oil until tender and put into pie shell. Mix remaining ingredients together except cheese and pour over onions. Top with grated cheese. Bake 45 minutes at 350 degrees. Serves 8.

Carolyn J. Finkle
Lubbock, TX

BEV'S VIDALIA ONION PIE

3　cups thinly sliced Vidalia
　　Sweet Onions
2　tablespoons melted butter
1　deep dish frozen pie crust,
　　thawed
½　cup milk
1½　cups light sour cream

3　tablespoons all-purpose flour
1　teaspoon salt
2　eggs, well beaten
　　Bacon strips, crisply fried and
　　crumbled, garnish
　　Chopped Parsley, garnish

Cook onions in melted butter until lightly browned. Spoon into the pie shell. Blend milk with 1¼ cups of light sour cream. Blend flour and salt with remaining ¼ cup of sour cream and combine both with the beaten egg. Pour over onions. Bake in slow 325 degree oven for 30 minutes or until firm in the center. Cool and garnish with crumbled bacon and chopped parsley. When preparing for the freezer, only partially bake the pie. To serve frozen pie, thaw and continue baking until center is firm and then garnish with bacon and parsley. Serves 6 to 8.

"This recipe is wonderful with grilled steaks and a tossed salad. It also freezes well."

Ellen Buckner
Chattanooga, TN

Mrs. G. Dana Waters, II
Birmingham, AL

CATHERINE'S ONION PIE

1   to 2 tablespoons oil
1½   jumbo or 3 large Vidalia
      Sweet Onions, sliced
2   tablespoons white cooking
      wine
2   eggs, beaten or ½ cup egg
      substitute
3   tablespoons chopped fresh
      parsley, divided

1   tablespoon chopped fresh dill
      or 1 teaspoon dried
½   teaspoon dried tarragon
      Pepper
4   ounces crumbled Feta cheese
      Fine dry bread crumbs

Heat oil in pan and sauté Vidalia sweet onions for 5 minutes. Add wine and continue to sauté till golden, approximately 15 minutes. Preheat oven to 350 degrees. Combine eggs with 2 tablespoons parsley, dill, tarragon, pepper and cheese. Stir in onions. Spray a 8 or 9-inch springform or tart pan with cooking spray and line bottom generously with crumbs. Pour in onion mixture and sprinkle with 1 tablespoon parsley and a light layer of crumbs. Bake 40 to 45 minutes until top is golden. Let stand 5 to 10 minutes before slicing.
Serves 6 to 8.

Catherine Johnson
Plains, MT

COMPANY CHEESE AND ONION PIE

1½   cups soda crackers, crushed
¼   cup melted butter or marga-
      rine plus 2 tablespoons,
      divided
2½   cups Vidalia Sweet Onions,
      thinly sliced
1¼   cups evaporated skim milk

3   eggs, slightly beaten
¾   teaspoon salt
½   teaspoon coarsely ground
      black pepper
1   8-ounce package Swiss
      cheese, chopped or grated

Mix cracker crumbs and butter together and press into a 9-inch pie plate. Sauté onions in 2 tablespoons butter until yellowish and tender but not brown. Spread onions over crust. Combine milk and eggs. Add salt, pepper and cheese. Stir well; pour over onions. Bake in 325 degree oven for 40 to 45 minutes or until knife inserted comes out clean. Serves 6 to 7.

Lettie C. Cardy
Normandy, TN

CINDY'S SUNDAY PIE (FOR TIRED GARDENERS!)

3	eggs	2	tablespoons sour cream
1	cup milk	8	ounces frozen asparagus
¾	cup prepared biscuit mix		spears
	Salt, to taste	⅔	cup canned sliced mush-
¼	teaspoon white pepper		rooms
1	teaspoon dried dill weed	1	jumbo Vidalia Sweet Onion
¼	cup grated Romano cheese		Paprika

Blend eggs, milk, biscuit mix, salt, pepper, dill weed, Romano cheese, and sour cream. Spray ceramic quiche pan with olive oil pan spray. Lay asparagus in spoke pattern on bottom of dish, cover with sliced mushrooms. Top with thin slices of onion, using the whole onion. Pour in blended mixture, sprinkle lightly with paprika. Cook in 325 degree oven for approximately 35 minutes until top is browned and puffy. Inserted knife in center will come out clean. Serves 3 hungry adults.
Note: Serve for Sunday supper with tossed salad, baby carrots in butter and grated orange rind. Offer a good, traditional, grainy French mustard on the side, and some Bland Farm peach preserves as a special treat!

Cynthia Vaida
Stanton, NJ

DELICIOUS VIDALIA SWEET ONION PIE

2½	pounds Vidalia Sweet Onions,	1	teaspoon salt
	thinly sliced	½	teaspoon pepper
3	tablespoons butter or oleo,	1	teaspoon dill or celery seed
	melted	1	9-inch pie shell, chilled
3	eggs	1	egg white
1	cup sour cream	4	strips bacon, diced

Add onions to butter. Stir and cook over low heat until translucent. Combine eggs, sour cream, and seasonings and stir into onions. Brush bottom of chilled pie shell with 1 slightly bean egg white. Fill with slightly cooled onion mixture. Place bacon on top. Bake in 450 degree oven for 10 minutes. Reduce heat to 300 degrees. Bake 30 minutes more. Absorb excess bacon grease with paper towel. Serve piping hot. Serves 6 to 8.

Jacqueline D. Andrews
Lakeland, FL

EDNA'S VIDALIA SWEET ONION PIE

3	cups thinly sliced Vidalia Sweet Onions	1¼	cups milk
			Salt and pepper
2	tablespoons butter or margarine	½	cup butter or margarine
		1½	cups saltine crackers
3	eggs, slightly beaten	½	cup grated Cheddar cheese

Sauté onions in 2 tablespoons butter. Cool slightly. Blend eggs and milk and season as desired with salt and pepper. Mix with onions. Mix cracker crumbs and ½ cup butter or margarine together and press into bottom and sides of 9-inch pie pan. Pour in onion mixture. Sprinkle with grated Cheddar cheese and bake at 350 degrees for 30 minutes or until center is firm. Serves 6 to 8.

"This freezes well."

Edna Lowell
El Cajon, CA

Variation: For smaller pie, use 2 medium onions, thinly sliced, 1 cup cracker crumbs, ¼ cup melted butter, ¾ cup milk, 2 eggs and ½ cup grated cheese. Follow directions above for preparing pie.

Janie Glass
Iowa Park, TX
Lorraine G. Labun
Agawam, MA

RUTH'S ONION PIE

1	9-inch unbaked pastry shell	2	eggs, beaten
2	cups chopped Vidalia Sweet Onion	1	teaspoon salt
			Black pepper, to taste
¼	cup butter	2	tablespoons finely chopped parsley
½	cup grated Swiss cheese plus		
1	tablespoon all purpose flour		

Sauté chopped onion in butter and put into unbaked pastry shell. Mix together cheese and flour. Add eggs, salt, pepper and parsley. Pour over onions. Bake at 375 degrees for 40 to 45 minutes or until knife comes clean. Serve warm.

Ruth S. Fortino
Bethlehem, PA

GEORGIA ONION PIE

8 tablespoons or 1 stick un-salted butter, divided	2 large egg yolks
5 cups thinly sliced Vidalia Sweet Onions	1 cup sour cream
1½ cups crushed round butter flavored crackers	¼ teaspoon grated nutmeg Salt and freshly ground white pepper, to taste
1½ tablespoons unbleached all-purpose flour	1½ cups shredded sharp Cheddar cheese
½ cup chicken broth	1 teaspoon sweet Hungarian paprika

Preheat oven to 350 degrees. Melt 4 tablespoons butter in a large skillet over medium heat. Add the onions and sauté, stirring occasionally, until quite soft and tender, about 20 minutes. Melt the remaining 4 tablespoons butter and toss with cracker crumbs to moisten thoroughly and press into bottom and up sides of 9-inch pie plate. Set aside. Stir flour into onions and cook 1 minute. Stir in chicken broth and cook until liquid is slightly thickened and creamy, about 2 minutes. Remove from heat. Whisk egg yolks and sour cream in a small mixing bowl until well blended. Season with nutmeg, salt, and white pepper. Add egg mixture to onions and stir to blend thoroughly. Pour the onion mixture into the pie plate. Top with Cheddar cheese, then sprinkle with paprika. Bake pie until lightly browned and bubbling, 35 to 40 minutes. Let cool 5 minutes. Slice pie into wedges, as best you can, and serve at once.
Serves 6 to 8.

Joseph F. Noonan
Norfolk, MA

SKILLIGALEE ONION PIE

1	refrigerated 9-inch deep dish pie crust	6	tablespoons sour cream
6	tablespoons butter		Salt, to taste
3	medium Vidalia Sweet Onions, sliced		Pepper, to taste
½	cup all purpose flour	1¼	cups shredded Cheddar cheese
2	cups whipping cream		

In a skillet, melt butter. Over medium heat, sauté onions until tender, but not brown, about 8 to 10 minutes. Sprinkle flour over and stir until onions are evenly coated. Stirring constantly, slowly pour in cream. Remove from heat. Add sour cream. Season to taste with salt and pepper. Pour into pie shell. Sprinkle cheese evenly over top. Bake at 350 degrees until crust is golden and cheese is melted and begins to brown, about 45 minutes. Let cool completely so it will be firm enough to slice, at least hour. If desired, preheat each portion 3 or 5 minutes just before serving. Serves 8.

Cathy Glatthar
King William, VA

VIDALIA SWEET ONION PIE

1	9-inch pastry shell, unbaked	2	eggs
3	cups sliced or cubed Vidalia Sweet Onions	½	cup evaporated milk
3	tablespoons butter or margarine	1	teaspoon salt
		⅛	teaspoon black pepper

Sauté onions in butter or margarine until tender. Arrange on pastry shell. Beat eggs slightly and add evaporated milk, salt and pepper. Pour mixture over onions. Bake in preheated 425 degree oven for 18 to 20 minutes, or until knife inserted near center comes out clean. Serves 4 to 6.

Bessie M. Stokes
Sun City, AZ

Betty Z. Doeringer
Plainfield, NJ

Ellen L. Brod
Worcester, MA

VIDALIA ONION PIE BY DREW

1	8-inch ready made pie crust		Salt and pepper, to taste
4	medium Vidalia Sweet Onions,	⅛	teaspoon tarragon
	peeled and sliced thin	4	slices bacon, diced
1	large egg, beaten		Dash paprika
½	cup half and half		

Peel the onions and slice thin. Blend beaten egg and half and half together. Season to taste with salt, pepper, and tarragon. Mix in onions. Place in pie crust and cover with diced bacon. Sprinkle paprika over the mixture. Bake in a moderate 350 degree oven for 35 minutes. When partially cooked, about 10 minutes, add just a little more cream on top of bacon. Cut in wedges and serve with almost any kind of meat. Serves 6.

Leon and Mary Drew
Laughlin, NV

VIDALIA SWEET ONION PIE WITH PARMESAN CHEESE

1	cup crushed soda crackers	Salt
¼	cup melted butter	Pepper
15	Baby Vidalia Sweet Onions	Parsley flakes
	(lemon sized)	Parmesan cheese
3	eggs (large or 4 small)	
1½	cups milk	

Line a large deep dish pie pan with a crust made of 1 cup crushed soda crackers and melted butter. Pat firmly into pan. Slice onions thinly. Sauté in butter until tender and pour into crust. Beat eggs with 1½ cups of milk and season with salt and pepper. Pour over onions. Put a border of parsley around edge and a row of Parmesan cheese next to parsley. Bake at 350 degrees for 45 to 60 minutes or until filling is set and knife comes out clean. Serve at once. Serves 8.

Mrs. George E. Keller
South Bend, IN

ZUCCHINI AND ONION PIE

3	cups zucchini, chopped or sliced	½	cup olive oil
2	Vidalia Sweet Onions, coarsely chopped	4	eggs, beaten
		1	teaspoon salt
1	cup prepared biscuit mix	½	teaspoon pepper
½	cup Parmesan cheese		Fresh or dry basil
			Dry parsley

Mix all ingredients together and pour into greased baking dish. Bake uncovered in 350 degree oven approximately 30 to 45 minutes. Test with knife inserted into center. Pie is done when knife comes out clean or pie is brown around edges. Serves 6 to 8.

"Compliment to steak or any fish entree or lunch entree."

Lucy M. Hudock
Riverside, CT

ZWIEBEL KUCHEN
(ONION PIE)

1½	cups sifted all purpose flour	½	cup milk
¾	teaspoon salt	1½	cups dairy sour cream, divided
1½	teaspoons caraway seeds		
½	cup shortening	1	teaspoon salt
2	to 3 tablespoons water	2	eggs, well beaten
3	cups peeled, thinly sliced Vidalia Sweet Onions	3	tablespoons flour
		5	slices bacon, cooked & crumbled (for garnish)
3	tablespoons melted oleo		

To prepare pie crust, combine flour, salt, caraway seeds, shortening together until crumbly. Add water and roll out to fit in 10-inch pie pan. Bake in 425 degree oven for 10 minutes. Sauté onions in oleo until lightly browned. Spoon into pie crust. In a bowl, add milk, 1¼ cups sour cream, salt and the well beaten eggs. Mix, then blend flour with remaining ¼ cup sour cream. Combine egg mixture to flour mixture and pour over onions in pie crust. Bake in slow 325 degree oven 30 minutes or until firm in center. Garnish with 5 slices crumbled, crisp, fried bacon. Serves 8.
Note: Zwiebel Kuchen is of German origin.

Helen E. Keeley
Phoenix, AZ

OMELET FOR DIETERS

Vidalia Sweet Onions   **Minced garlic**
Fresh mushrooms   **Egg substitute**

Dice onion. Cook in omelet frying pan or any fat substitute until soft. Clean and cut fresh mushrooms and add to onions. Add garlic to taste. Cook until well done. Pour egg substitute over and let cook until well set. Flip over half way. Finish cooking until done.

Diced ham, diced peppers, pimentos, or diet cheese can be added. Serves 2.

Alice Stiewing
Waterbury, CT

SUPPER OMELET FOR TWO

½   **Vidalia Sweet Onion, sliced**   2   **ounces canned mushrooms**
½   **bell pepper, sliced**   3   **eggs**
2   **tablespoons oil**   **Herbal seasonings**

Sauté onion and peppers in oil until onion is transparent and pepper is tender. Add mushrooms and heat through. Beat eggs and pour over vegetables, then add seasonings. Cover and cook over low heat until eggs are set. Fold over carefully. Cut in half.

Top with salsa of your choice before serving. Serve with garlic bread and a green salad. Serves 2.

"This recipe was one of my mother-in-law's favorite. Only she prepared it for large crowds."

Helen Lordi
Baldwin Park, CA

CHILI PEPPER~VIDALIA ONION QUICHE

1	9" deep dish ready made pie crust	½	pound lowfat Ricotta cheese
2	medium Vidalia Sweet Onions, chopped	1	cup grated Colby and Monterey Jack cheese, mixed
2	tablespoons lowfat oleo	1	4 1/2 ounce green chilies, chopped
3	eggs, beaten		
¼	cup half and half	½	teaspoon salt
½	cup lowfat sour cream	¼	teaspoon fresh pepper
		¼	teaspoon nutmeg, divided

Prepare pie crust following package instructions. Sauté onions in oleo. Mix together eggs, half and half, sour cream, cheeses, green chilies, salt and pepper and ⅛ teaspoon nutmeg. Add onions. Mix together. Pour into pie crust and bake 10 minutes at 450 degrees. Sprinkle ⅛ teaspoon nutmeg over top and bake 1 hour in 350 degree oven. Reduce cooking time to 40 minutes for lower altitudes.

Lora Lee Rosner
Cheyenne, WY

VIDALIA ONION QUICHE

1	9-inch pie crust	2	cups (8-ounces) shredded Swiss cheese
4	tablespoons (¼ cup or ½ stick) butter	1	egg plus 2 yolks
¼	cup water	¾	cup heavy cream
2	large Vidalia Sweet Onions	⅛	teaspoon nutmeg
	Salt		
	White pepper		

Bake pricked pie crust at 450 degrees for 10 to 12 minutes. Cool. Slice onions thinly and simmer about 10 minutes with water and butter. Drain well. Add salt and pepper, then put into pie crust. Sprinkle with cheese. Beat together eggs, cream, and nutmeg; pour over onions and bake at 375 degrees for 45 minutes. Serves 6 to 8.

"This quiche may be served hot or cold as hors d'oeuvre cut into bite sized pieces."

Jan Hummon
Farmington Hill, MI

ONION AND CHEESE QUICHE

1	9-inch unbaked pie shell	3	tablespoons butter
½	pint whipping cream	1	tablespoon vegetable oil
4	eggs	½	cup grated Swiss or Gruyere
	Dash of nutmeg		cheese
2	dashes salt and pepper		
4	medium sized Vidalia Sweet Onions		

Bake pie shell in 450 degree oven for 5 minutes. Remove and set aside. Reduce oven heat to 375 degrees. Combine whipping cream, eggs, nutmeg, salt, and pepper, beating until smooth. Slice onions into thin rings and sauté in butter and oil until limp but not brown. Spread onions in the partially baked pie shell; add grated cheese, then pour cream mixture over cheese and onions. It will fill pie shell to the top. Bake on cookie sheet at 375 degrees for about 30 minutes or until tip is lightly browned and a knife inserted in the custard comes out clean. Allow the pie to rest before cutting. Serves 4 to 6.

"For extra richness, 2 extra egg yolks may be added when adding the 4 eggs. Some recipes say to cook onions slowly for an hour, but this quiche tastes good even if you don't do that. You can even put the onions in raw."

Betty Woodward
Fairfax, VA

BLUE CHEESE AND ONION TART

1   cup unbleached all purpose
     flour
     Salt, pinch
1   egg yolk
8   tablespoons unsalted butter
4   tablespoons ice water
1½   tablespoons unsalted butter
4½   cups thinly sliced Vidalia
     Sweet Onion

1   cup crumbled Blue cheese
3   large eggs
¼   cup cream
½   cup milk
     Salt, to taste
     Freshly ground pepper, to
       taste
2   shallots

To make pastry, place flour and pinch of salt in a medium bowl. Make a well, add egg yolk and cut in 8 tablespoons butter. Mix together with fingertips until butter is softened. Add water to well and mix. Very gradually add flour mixture to liquids and mix dough until it holds together. It may be crumbly, do not over mix. Preheat oven to 400 degrees. For filling, melt 1½ tablespoons butter in large skillet over medium heat. When butter foams, add onions and stir. Cover skillet, reduce heat to low and cook until golden for 20 minutes, stirring. Add blue cheese to onions, stir until melted. Season with salt and pepper to taste. Roll out dough to fit 10-inch tart or quiche pan. Bake crust in oven for 12 to 15 minutes. In small bowl, mix eggs, cream and milk. Season with salt and pepper to taste. Slice shallots into paper thin slices. Pour onion and blue cheese mixture into pan. Pour cream mixture over all. Arrange shallot slices on top. Bake 25 to 30 minutes until golden and puffed.
Serves 6.
Note: Phyllo dough sheets may be substituted for tart pastry.

Mr. and Mrs. T. Schneider
Mahwah, NJ

Pickles, Relishes & Sauces

BLUE CHEESE AND ONIONS

1½ ounces of crumbled Blue
       cheese
¼   cup salad oil
½   teaspoon salt

¼   teaspoon sugar
1½ tablespoons lemon juice
2   large Vidalia Sweet Onions,
       sliced into rings

Mix cheese, oil, salt, sugar, and lemon juice. Pour over onion rings. Chill several hours. Yields 3 cups.

Donna Jennings
Hawley, PA

DILLED CUCUMBERS AND ONIONS

¾   cup sour cream
2   tablespoons cider vinegar
1   rounded teaspoon dill seed
1½ teaspoons salt

⅛   teaspoon pepper
1   tablespoon sugar
3   large cucumbers
2   large Vidalia Sweet Onions

Mix sour cream, vinegar, dill seed, salt, pepper and sugar together and pour on sliced cucumbers and onions. Best if allowed to stand overnight.

Maxine Ours
Butler, MO

DILLY ONION RINGS

1   large or 3 small Vidalia
       Sweet Onions
⅓   cup sugar
2   teaspoons salt

1   teaspoon dried dill weed
½   cup white vinegar
¼   cup water

Cut onion into thin slices. Separate into rings. Combine sugar, salt, dill weed, vinegar and water. Stir until sugar is dissolved. Pour over onion rings. Cover tightly in jar and refrigerate at least 5 hours. Shake occasionally.
Yields one 8-ounce jar.

Mrs. John E. Berg
Flossmoor, IL

DUTCH CUCUMBER AND ONIONS

1   large Vidalia Sweet Onion,   ½   cup vinegar
    sliced thinly   ½   cup water
1   large or medium cucumber,   1   teaspoon salt
    peeled and sliced thinly   Pepper
½   cup sugar

Combine above ingredients and chill 4 hours before serving.

Lois E. Larsen
Las Vegas, NV

DIANE'S MARINATED ONIONS

4   to 6 cups Vidalia Sweet   ¼   cup olive oil
    Onions   4   tablespoons tarragon vinegar
1   teaspoon dried crushed   Salt
    oregano   Pepper
½   teaspoon dried crushed basil

Slice onions into ¼-inch rings, or finer if preferred, and toss with rest of ingredients. Put into a zip-lock plastic bag and toss occasionally. Should be made up to 2 hours ahead of serving or early in the day and kept refrigerated. Bring to room temperature at least 1 hour before serving.
Note: Great served with hot dogs and baked beans or on a buffet.

Diane Hagopian
Waukegan, IL

LORI'S MARINATED ONIONS

2	large or 3 small Vidalia Sweet Onions	¼	cup oil
¼	cup vinegar	½	cup catsup

Cut up onions to fill quart jar. Stir vinegar, oil, and catsup together until well blended. Pour over onions. Refrigerate and let marinate for 24 hours before serving.
Note: Enjoy with meats, sandwiches, or nearly any other food.

Lori Anne Lamb
Slaton, TX

MARINATED CUCUMBER AND VIDALIA SWEET ONIONS

1	cup cider vinegar		Pepper, to taste
¾	cup water, to taste	2	cucumbers, sliced thin
½	cup sugar	1	Vidalia Sweet Onion, sliced thin
	Salt, to taste		

Combine vinegar, water, sugar, salt and pepper and pour over cucumbers and onion. Let stand 30 minutes for flavors to blend.

Desi L. Andis
San Jose, CA

MARINATED VIDALIA ONIONS

2	cups water	2	or 3 Vidalia Sweet Onions, sliced
1	cup sugar		
½	cup vinegar	1	cup mayonnaise
	Celery seed		Salt

Bring water, sugar, vinegar, and celery seed to a boil and pour over onions. Cover and let stand 20 minutes. Drain well, stir mayonnaise into onions. Let stand in refrigerator 24 hours before serving. Serves 6 to 8.

Mrs. Tilman Ogburn
Alexander City, AL

MARINATED VIDALIA SWEET ONIONS

2	cups water	½	cup mayonnaise
3	cups white vinegar, optional	1	tablespoon celery seed
3	tablespoons sugar		Freshly ground black pepper
3	to 4 white Vidalia Sweet Onions, thinly sliced and separated into rings		Green peppercorns
			Salt

Heat water and vinegar in a medium sauce pan until the solutions seems warm. Add sugar and heat until sugar is dissolved. Soak onions covered in this marinade overnight. Drain well. In a medium bowl, mix mayonnaise, celery seed, pepper, green peppercorns and salt. Stir the onion into this mixture and serve cool.

"These onions are delicious with cold roast beef."

Mrs. Burt Pharis
Newark, OH

PEGGY'S MARINATED ONIONS

1	large cucumber	1	teaspoon salt
⅓	cup vinegar	¼	teaspoon pepper
2	tablespoons water		Vidalia Sweet Onions, sliced
¼	cup sugar	1	tablespoon minced dill

Peel cucumber and slice thin. Place slices in ice water, refrigerate for 1 hour and drain. Combine vinegar, water, sugar, salt and pepper and pour over cucumber and sliced Vidalia sweet onion. Refrigerate at least 1 hour. At serving time drain off liquid and serve. Sprinkle with dill. Serves 4.

Peggy DeRosear
Hamilton, IL

LENA'S PICKLED ONIONS

2 cups water
1 cup cider vinegar
½ cup sugar
2 tablespoons mixed pickling
  spice, tied in a spice bag

½ teaspoon crushed red
  peppers
2 teaspoons salt
8 medium Vidalia Sweet Onions

In a 4-quart sauce pan, bring all ingredients to a boil. Simmer uncovered for 10 minutes. Refrigerate until chilled. Remove spice bag. Put in containers and refrigerate.
Note: Will keep in refrigerator 2 weeks or longer. Goes well with all dishes.

Mrs. Michael J. Pronko
Dalhart, TX

REFRIGERATOR CUKES AND ONIONS

4 cups thinly sliced cucumbers
2½ cups thinly sliced Vidalia
   Sweet Onions
1 cup thinly sliced sweet bell
  pepper

2 cups sugar
1 cup cider vinegar
1 tablespoon celery seed
1 teaspoon salt

Slice vegetables and set aside. Stir sugar, vinegar, salt, celery seed until dissolved. Pour over sliced vegetables and store in refrigerator. Will keep up to a week.

Lena Dahmer
Nevada, MO

ONION~LEMON CHUTNEY

6	large Vidalia Sweet Onions	1	cup white wine vinegar
2	medium size lemons	3	tablespoons finely chopped
¾	cup currants		fresh ginger
1½	cups sugar	¼	teaspoon ground allspice

Cut onions in half lengthwise and slice thinly. In a 5 to 6-quart pan, cover and cook onions in their own juices over medium heat , stirring occasionally until onions are limp, about 10 to 15 minutes. Cut lemons in half lengthwise, then slice thinly. Remove all seeds. Add lemons, currants, sugar, vinegar, ginger and all spice to onions. Simmer uncovered stirring often as it thickens. Cook until most of liquid has evaporated, approximately 1 hour. Seal in jars and process, or cool, cover and chill up to 1 month.

Note: To process for canning, ladle hot chutney into clean, hot, sterilized ½-pint canning jars to within ¼-inch of rim. Run a narrow spatula down between food and jar to release air bubbles. Wipe jar rims clean. Cover with hot sterilized lids; screw on bands. Place jars on rack in deep kettle half full of hot water. Add more hot water to cover jars by 1 to 2-inches. Bring water to simmering. Cover kettle, process for 10 minutes. Lift out jars and cool on a towel.

Jeanette Sharpsteen
Palos Verdes Estates, CA

BAKED ONION/APPLE RELISH

8	large cooking applies, sliced	½	teaspoon salt
8	large Vidalia Sweet Onions, sliced in rings		Crumbs, cracker or day old bread
7	tablespoons brown sugar	4	tablespoons butter (½ stick)

Butter a deep 2½-quart casserole. Put in a layer of apples, then add a layer of onions. Sprinkle with ½ of the sugar and a bit of salt. Repeat twice more ending with sugar and salt. Dish should be heaping. Contents will cook down. Top with crumbs and thinly sliced butter. Bake at 300 degrees for 3 hours, covered. Uncover last half hour to brown crumbs. Mixture should be dark and caramelized. Serves 8.

"This dish must be tasted to be appreciated. Delicious and so easy."

Donna Lee Herold
Los Osos, CA

ONION RELISH

2	large Vidalia Sweet Onions	¼	teaspoon freshly grated pepper
2	lemons		
⅓	cup sugar		

Chop onions finely and add juice of 2 lemons, sugar, and pepper. Mix well. Cover and refrigerate at least 2 hours. Drain well and it is ready to serve. Serves 12.

"This recipe is a wonderful accompaniment for any kind of meat. Also it is great for a picnic to use on hot dogs or hamburgers."

Mabelle Vosteen
Redlion, PA

VIDALIA SWEET ONION PARMESAN RELISH

1	medium Vidalia Sweet Onion, diced	2	tablespoons chopped green pepper
10	ripe cherry tomatoes, cut in half	2	tablespoons chopped yellow pepper
2	tablespoons chopped celery hearts	2	tablespoons frozen baby green peas, thawed
2	tablespoons chopped red pepper	1	teaspoon Parmesan cheese, grated

Toss all vegetables together in a large mixing bowl. Sprinkle cheese on top and stir slightly. Cover and refrigerate for at least 2 hours. Serves 6 to 8.

Note: This can be made one day in advance. Serve over grilled chicken or pork or as a salad on a spinach or lettuce leaf.

"Frequently asked question: what is the substitute for Vidalias? Answer: I always have them."

Darlene McCoy
Cleveland, OH

VIDALIA SWEET ONION RELISH

1	tablespoon pickling spices	1	cup chopped green pepper
⅓	cup water	¼	teaspoon black pepper
⅓	cup cider vinegar	1	cup chopped ripe tomatoes
2	tablespoons sugar	2	cups thinly sliced Vidalia Sweet Onions
¾	teaspoon salt		

Tie pickling spices in cheesecloth. In medium saucepan, heat spice bag and remaining ingredients except the onions. Bring to a boil. Reduce heat to medium, add onions and cook an additional 5 minutes. Remove spice bag. Place in bowl, cover and refrigerate. Serves 8 to 10.

It is easy to double the recipe several times over and make a larger quantity. Place in clean sterilized jars, cover tightly and refrigerate. Keeps for months. Great on hamburgers.

Helga Schlape
Florham Park, NJ

ZESTY ONION ~ CORN RELISH

1   cup minced Vidalia Sweet Onion
1   11-ounce can corn, drained
½   teaspoon dry mustard

1   tablespoon apple cider vinegar
1   tablespoon olive oil
Salt and pepper, to taste

Combine onion and corn in large bowl. Add mustard and stir with fork to mix all ingredients. Add vinegar and oil. Stir with fork until onion - corn mixture is coated with liquid. Add salt and pepper to taste. Serves 4.
Note: Terrific accompaniment to grilled burgers, steaks and chops.

Marilyn R. Block
Bethesda, MD

VIDALIA SWEET ONIONS IN DILL SAUCE

⅓   cup mayonnaise
1   tablespoon cider vinegar
1   tablespoon water

½   teaspoon sugar
½   teaspoon salt, optional
1   teaspoon chopped dill
1   large Vidalia Sweet Onion

Mix mayonnaise, vinegar, water, and sugar in medium bowl. Add salt, if desired, and dill. Stir well to avoid small lumps. Slice Vidalia sweet onion to ¼ - inch thick and add to first mixture. Refrigerate at least 1 hour before serving to let flavors develop. Serves 4.
Note: Will keep 3 to 4 days.

Helen A. Taylor
Clearwater, FL

HOT VIDALIA SWEET ONION DIPPING SAUCE

3	Vidalia sweet onions, sliced	1	tablespoon lemon juice
5	pomodoro tomatoes, small sliced (or Roma)	1	teaspoon Italian herbs
		¾	teaspoon salt
1	cup olive oil	1	tablespoon cracked black pepper

Cook above in microwave until done. Store in refrigerator.

"Dipping sauce for French bread or cubed cheese."

Marilyn Geraty
Sacramento, CA

VIDALIA SWEET ONION SAUCE

1	tablespoon butter or margarine	2	tablespoons white or cider vinegar
2	cups sliced Vidalia sweet onions	2	tablespoons sugar
		¼	cup water

Melt butter in large frying pan. Sauté sliced onions until softened. Add vinegar, sugar, and water and stir well. Cook for 15 minutes on low heat. Yields 2 cups.

Note: This sauce can be used on hot dogs, hamburgers, grilled meats, and on chicken.

Marylee Pratnicki
Long Beach, NJ

ONIONS IN MUSTARD SAUCE

1	cup corn oil	¼	teaspoon fresh ground black
1	cup cider vinegar		pepper
1	teaspoon dry mustard	1	tablespoon sugar
¼	teaspoon poultry seasoning	3	medium Vidalia Sweet Onions
¼	teaspoon salt		

In wide-mouth mason jar put all ingredients except onions. Screw cap on and shake well. Let settle. Slice onions ⅛-inch to ¼-inch thick. Place onions slightly separated into rings in jar. Push down gently with wooden spoon. If the jar will hold more onions, being sure they are immersed in marinade, by all means add more. Marinate at least 2 days. Yields 1 quart.

"Use as topping on salads, on hamburgers, with slices of broiled steak or lamb, in rolls or any way you please."

Ann M.C. Kittredge
Tremonton, UT

ONION AND MUSHROOM WINE SAUCE

1	stick butter (1/2 cup)	¾	cup white port wine
1	large Vidalia Sweet Onion,	¼	cup honey
	coarsely chopped	½	teaspoon salt
1	cup sliced mushrooms, sliced		
	¼-inch thick		

Melt butter and add onion. Lightly sauté for 5 minutes, add mushrooms and bring back to simmer. Add wine, honey, and salt. Simmer on very low heat for about 10 minutes. Serve immediately. Serves 4.

"This recipe is very good served with charbroiled steak as a side dish or poured over the steak as a sauce. Even good on mashed potatoes."

James H. Weidman
Huntingtown, MD

Special Vidalia Sweet Onion Treats

B L A N D   F A R M S

BARBECUED ONIONS

12	Baby Vidalia Sweet Onions	1	tablespoon molasses
¾	cup ketchup	2	tablespoons brown sugar
½	cup water	1	teaspoon Worcestershire
4	tablespoons butter		sauce
2	tablespoons finely minced Vidalia sweet onion	1	teaspoon prepared mustard

Peel onions and cut a small cross in root end. Boil gently until barely tender. Drain and put in buttered casserole dish. Put remaining ingredients in a saucepan and cook over low heat for 30 minutes. Pour over onions and bake, uncovered at 350 degrees for 30 minutes. Serves 4.

"Ingredients for sauce can be adjusted to suit your taste. Excellent accompaniment for any beef or chicken dish."

Elizabeth H. Kinney
Newton, NJ

BARBECUE SIDE DISH

4	Vidalia Sweet Onions	Cooking spray
2	bell peppers, 1 green and 1 red	Pepper
	Garlic or celery salt	

Slice onions and peppers about ¼-inch thick. Sprinkle lightly with seasonings and toss with cooking spray. Put into frying pan on low heat and cook until onions and peppers are done. Dust with pepper. Allow 1 onion per person. Serves 4.

"The onions are a delight."

Frances Wright
Hemet, CA

CARAMELIZED VIDALIA SWEET ONIONS OVER PASTA

4	to 5 medium Vidalia Sweet Onions, peeled and cut in chunks	½	cup water
		1	package fresh cheese ravioli, or substitute a favorite pasta, cooked according to package directions

Spray a teflon-coated skillet with cooking spray and turn flame on high. Add onions, which will begin to sear immediately. Stir quickly until all sides are coated. Add water and cover. Keep watching and stir every few minutes. After 10 minutes, turn heat down to medium. Add a little more water if needed. For the next 30 minutes check and stir periodically; you don't want them sticking to the pan. The secret in caramelizing is to cook them slowly. Then remove lid so liquid can cook down while you're boiling the pasta. These onions will reduce to about 1½ cups of the sweetest and most buttery sauce you've ever made. Serve over ravioli or your favorite pasta. Serves 2.

Beverly McGuire
Hollywood, CA

CHRYSANTHEMUM ONIONS

1	Vidalia Sweet Onion per serving	1½	teaspoons balsamic vinegar per onion
1	tablespoon olive oil per person		Salt and pepper

Trim the root ends carefully so the onion will not break apart. Peel onions. Stand them on root ends and cut slices through the length of the onion, to within ½-inch of root, at ¼-inch intervals. Turn onion and cut slices to form a criss-cross pattern of ¼-inch squares. Soak 2 to 4 hours in ice water to blossom. Drain on paper towels. To grill or bake, place each onion on a square of foil, drizzle with the oil and vinegar and sprinkle with salt and pepper. Bring edges of foil together and crimp to seal. May be prepared 2 hours before cooking. Grill over glowing coals 20 to 25 minutes or bake until tender. To microwave do not use foil. Place onions in a microwave casserole, cover with waxed paper and microwave at full power 7 to 12 minutes depending on number of onions. Allow 1 onion per serving.

Helene Harned
Zionsville, PA

GRILLED VIDALIA SWEET ONIONS

1	medium Vidalia Sweet Onion per person	1	tablespoon balsamic vinegar per Vidalia Sweet Onion
1	tablespoon olive oil per Vidalia Sweet Onion		Salt Pepper

Place whole peeled Vidalia sweet onion in microwave on a paper towel. Microwave 3 to 5 minutes on HIGH or until onions are partially cooked. Pour 1 tablespoon oil and 1 tablespoon vinegar over each Vidalia sweet onion. Sprinkle salt and pepper over each. Let marinate at room temperature for 30 minutes or longer. Grill onions over hot coals, turning frequently. Serve warm or at room temperature.

Debra Reid
Carlisle, PA

Variation: Heat grill. Slice onions and place on grill until perfectly cooked.

Roz Bernheimer and daughters
Waban, MA

GREAT GRILLED VIDALIA SWEET ONIONS

1	Vidalia Sweet Onion Butter or margarine	Worcestershire sauce

Peel and halve onion crosswise. Slice a thin section from the root and top ends of the halves so they will lie flat. Place a pat, ½-tablespoon, of butter or margarine in the center of each half. Shake 2 to 3 dashes of Worcestershire sauce on top of the buttered onion. Place on the barbeque grill along with steaks, burgers, etc. Cook about 15 minutes until hot throughout but still crunchy. Do not turn. Serve alongside grilled entrees. You may baste with additional Worcestershire sauce during cooking and time may be increased if you prefer softer onion.

"Onions may also be cooked under the oven broiler for 8 to 10 minutes if you can't use the grill."

Donna Mistr
Jarrettsville, MD

GRILLED ONIONS

	Vidalia Sweet Onions		**Pepper, to taste**
1	**tablespoon butter**	2	**half slices bacon**
	Salt, to taste		

Pare large Vidalia sweet onions and remove a thin slice from the top and bottom. Make 4 cuts ¾ of the way through each onion from top to bottom forming 8 uniform wedges. Carefully cut out center of onions to depth of one inch. Place a tablespoon of butter in hollow and sprinkle with salt and pepper. Criss-cross 2 half slices of bacon over each onion. Wrap each in foil and bake in covered grill over ash gray coals. Cooking time will be about 45 minutes or until tender over direct heat. To serve, remove bacon and place under onion. Carefully unfold onion wedges to fashion flower.

Marian Sullivan
Oshkosh, WI

Variation: Slice tops off of Vidalia sweet onions to create flat surface. Cut an X into the flat top several layers deep and place a pat of butter on the X. Wrap a slice of bacon around the onion and over the X. Wrap each bacon wrapped onion in aluminum foil. Place on covered grill and grill for 30 to 45 minutes.

Jay F. Morris
Adelphi, MD

MICROWAVE VIDALIA SWEET ONIONS

3	**large Vidalia Sweet Onions, sliced ¼-inch thick**	3	**tablespoons butter or margarine**
3	**to 4 tablespoons water**		**Salt**
			Pepper

Slice Vidalia sweet onion about ¼-inch thick and place in covered microwave casserole dish. Add 3 tablespoons water. Cook on HIGH for 8 to 10 minutes or until tender, adding a little more water if needed. Remove and add butter, salt, and pepper to taste. Serves 4.

"This dish is delicious served with steaks or meat of your choice."

Mrs. Bessie S. Lanthrip
Mechanicsville, VA

NANCY'S BOURBON ONIONS

2	tablespoons butter	1	teaspoon salt
4	tablespoons olive oil	½	teaspoon pepper
4	large Vidalia Sweet Onions, sliced 1-inch thick	¼	cup bouillon
		¼	cup bourbon

Heat butter and oil in heavy saucepan. Add onions and sear over high heat for 2 minutes. Add salt, pepper, and bouillon. Reduce heat and simmer for 10 to 12 minutes. Add bourbon and cook down for 3 minutes. Serves 4 to 6.

"Wonderful with steak."

Nancy McKelvy
Williamsburg, VA

PARTY RATATOUILLE

3	large Vidalia Sweet Onions, sliced	¼	cup red French dressing
4	green peppers, cut into 1-inch pieces	1	clove garlic, minced
		¼	cup water
5	medium zucchini, sliced into ¼-inch thick	½	teaspoon oregano
		½	teaspoon salt
1	medium eggplant, sliced ¼-inch thick		Dash of pepper
		1	tablespoon Parmesan cheese
5	medium tomatoes, sliced	1	tablespoon dried parsley
2	cups, 8-ounces, grated Mozzarella cheese		

Place alternate layers of onion, peppers, zucchini, eggplant, tomatoes and Mozzarella in two 11¾x7½-inch baking dishes. Heat French dressing. Sauté garlic until lightly browned. Remove from heat. Stir in water and seasonings. Pour over casserole. Combine Parmesan cheese and parsley. Sprinkle over casserole. Bake at 350 degrees approximately 1½-hours. Serves 16 to 20.

Virginia R. Ross
Shrewsbury, MA

THE QUICKIE

Large Vidalia Sweet Onions **Butter**
Soy sauce

Peel and leave whole one large Vidalia sweet onion per person. Make several cuts across top of onion half way through. Spoon 2 or 3 tablespoons soy sauce over top. Place ½ teaspoon butter on top. Place in microwave on HIGH 6 to 9 minutes or until tender. Serves one onion per guest.

Robert R. Snow
Annandale, VA

SAVORY VIDALIA ONION TURNOVERS

1   **8-ounce package cream**   ½   **cup fresh mushrooms**
    cheese, softened   ½   **cup Cheddar cheese, grated**
1½ **cups Vidalia Sweet Onions,** ½   **cup crab meat, shredded**
    chopped fine   1   **package of Won Ton**
1   **scallion, chopped**   **wrappers**

Combine cream cheese, Vidalia sweet onions, scallion, mushrooms, Cheddar cheese and crab meat. Mix well. Spoon a heaping tablespoon of mixture in the center of a Won Ton wrapper. Fold over one side wetting the edges with water to seal. Bend the edges around. Deep fry until golden brown. Serve warm.

Carla DeFore
Byron, GA
First Place Winner
Georgia National Fair

SAUTÉED ONIONS WITH CATSUP

10   to 12 Vidalia Sweet Onions   6   to 8 tablespoons margarine
4   to 6-ounces catsup   or butter

In a large frying pan, sauté onions in 6 to 8 tablespoons of margarine. Add catsup after onions are sautéed and stir until catsup is completely dissolved into onions. Serves 4 to 6

"More catsup may be added to suit your taste. Can be prepared ahead of time and heated in microwave. Serve hot with steak and baked potato. We always cook this when we're camping."

Jean Cary
Pearl River, NY

SAUTÉED VIDALIA SWEET ONIONS AND MUSHROOMS

½   stick margarine (¼ cup)   ½   teaspoon onion powder
2   large Vidalia Sweet Onions   Salt
1   cup sliced mushrooms   Pepper
½   teaspoon garlic, minced or
         fresh

Melt margarine in skillet. Add rest of ingredients and simmer for approximately 20 minutes, or until all moisture is gone. Serves 2 to 3.
Note: Serve with steak or hamburgers.

Nina Barrett
Grandview, MO

SAUTÉED ONIONS WITH ORZO

4	tablespoons butter or oleo	¾	cup grated Swiss cheese
8	cups coarsely chopped Vidalia Sweet Onions	¾	cup orzo, raw
			Milk to thin mixture
			Salt and pepper, to taste

Sauté onions lightly in butter or margarine and stir often. Do not brown. Add Swiss cheese and stir in. Boil orzo for 8 minutes. Add cooked orzo to mixture; stir in and add milk as necessary to thin a bit. Salt and pepper.
Serves 6.

"We used this recipe all during Vidalia season. It is simple and delicious."

Mrs. John Boynton
Mequan, WI

SAUTÉED VIDALIA ONIONS

4	medium Vidalia sweet onions		Pepper, to taste
½	stick butter or margarine (¼ cup)		Sugar, pinch
	Salt, to taste	½	cup dry red wine

Slice onions, cook slowly in butter with salt, pepper and sugar for ½ hour. Add wine, cook again until thick. Serves 4.

"To accompany roast meat or liver."

Edith Nash
Wisconsin Rapids, WI

SHERRY GLAZED VIDALIA ONIONS

5	cups Vidalia Sweet Onion slices, sliced ¼-inch	¼	cup sherry
		2	tablespoons melted butter
3	tablespoons honey	1	tablespoon chopped parsley

Heat oven to 350 degrees. Separate onion slices into rings. Place in casserole dish. Combine honey, sherry, and melted butter. Pour over onion tossing until well coated. Cover and bake at 350 degrees for 25 minutes. Uncover and bake 15 minutes longer. Sprinkle with chopped parsley before serving. Serves 5.

Mrs. Ada Mahard
Natick, MA

SHERRIED GOURMET ONIONS

5	medium Vidalia Sweet Onions	½	teaspoon salt
⅓	cup butter, melted	½	teaspoon pepper
½	cup sherry		Almonds, slivered or sliced
2	tablespoons Parmesan cheese		

Slice onions into thin rings. Mix together the next 5 ingredients and pour over onion rings in a casserole. Top with almonds. Bake uncovered at 350 degrees for 25 minutes. Serve hot. Serves 4 to 6.

"Excellent with chicken and pork. We love those Vidalia onions and are so thrilled that we saw your ad in The Wall Street Journal. My husband and I are North Carolina transplants in Michigan, and the spring would not be the same without Vidalias hanging in knotted stockings!"

Laura Graham
Lansing, MI

STEAMED VIDALIA "PEE WEES" IN SWEET WHITE SAUCE

5	to 6 Pee Wees or medium Vidalia Sweet Onions	3	tablespoons all purpose flour
	Salt, to taste	1	teaspoon sugar or ½ pack artificial sweetener
¼	cup margarine	1	cup lowfat milk

Peel Vidalia sweet onions and place in microwave safe dish with only a few drops of water; sprinkle lightly with salt. Cover and steam until tender, about 8 to 10 minutes, depending on size of onions and your particular microwave. While onions are steaming, prepare white sauce by melting margarine over low heat in a pan or dish large enough to hold the Vidalias; add flour and sugar. If using sweetener, add it after sauce is finished. When mixture is bubbly and blended; use wire whip while adding milk. Stir with wire whip over low heat just until thickened. Pour juice which has accumulated from steaming Vidalias into white sauce to thin sauce if needed. Drop steamed Vidalias into sauce without further cooking. Serve with sauce in serving dish, or Vidalias on serving plates and spoon extra sauce over Vidalias. Serves 2 to 3.

"For variation, sprinkle sharp cheese on each serving."

Sara Nelle Warr
East Ellijay, GA

TAMALE SANDWICH WITH VIDALIA SWEET ONIONS

French or Italian sub buns,
  one per sandwich
Garlic spread with parsley
  and mixed herbs
Mustard
Tamale, one per sandwich

Medium Vidalia Sweet Onion,
  chopped
Sweet pepper, chopped
Chopped dill pickle relish

Steam tamale and set aside. Slice sub bun but not all the way through. Spread with garlic spread. Place in oven at 350 degrees for 10 minutes. Spread mustard on one side. Remove tamale from wrapper and place in bun. Put a generous amount of Vidalia sweet onion on tamale. Add chopped dill pickle relish and chopped sweet pepper.

"This is a favorite sandwich of men and teenage boys. The girls like it too but swear it is too big for them, but they finish the sandwich."

Eleanore A. Belt
Chicago Heights, IL

THE ULTIMATE ONION

3   cups cornstarch
1½   cups all purpose flour
2   teaspoons garlic salt
2   teaspoons paprika
1   teaspoon salt
1   teaspoon pepper

24   ounces beer
4   to 6 large Vidalia Sweet
       Onions, 4" in diameter or
       larger
Seasoned flour
1   quart creamy chili sauce

Mix cornstarch, flour and seasonings until well blended. Add beer, mix well. Cut about ¾-inch off top of onion; peel onion. Cut onion into 12 to 16 vertical wedges, but do not cut through bottom. Remove about 1-inch of "petals" from center of onion. Dip onion in seasoned flour and remove excess by shaking; dip in batter and remove excess by gently shaking. Separate "petals" to coat thoroughly with batter. Mix batter after standing to blend ingredients. Gently place in fryer basket and deep fry at 375 to 400 degrees for 1½ minutes. Turn over and fry 1 to 1½ minute longer or until golden brown. Recipe for seasoned flour and creamy chili sauce on page 183. Serves 4 to 6.

National Onion Association
Greeley, CO

SEASONED FLOUR

2	cups flour	½	teaspoon pepper
4	teaspoons paprika	¼	teaspoon cayenne pepper
2	teaspoons garlic powder		

Combine all ingredients and mix well. Use with THE ULTIMATE ONION Recipe on page 182.

National Onion Association
Greely, CO

CREAMY CHILI SAUCE

1	pint mayonnaise	½	cup chili sauce
1	pint dairy sour cream	½	teaspoon cayenne pepper

Combine all ingredients together. Keep chilled. Use with THE ULTIMATE ONION recipe on page 182.

National Onion Association
Greeley, CO

UNCLE BOB'S ENHANCED VIDALIAS

1	good sized Vidalia Sweet Onion	2	tablespoons bourbon or dry white vermouth
1	tablespoon corn or canola oil		

Peel and slice onion, separate into circles, and place in sauté pan or skillet with the cooking oil. Sauté over medium heat, stirring until onions are just becoming translucent. Remove from heat, add 2 tablespoons of bourbon or vermouth. Cover tightly and let cool. If onions are to be served with hot food, serve warm. If for use in salads, place in covered container with juices and refrigerate. Vermouth Vidalias are best for salads or mixed with other warm vegetables. Bourbon Vidalias go best with meats or grilled fish. Serves 2 to 4.

Robert N. Kharasch
Washington, DC

VIDALIA DELICIOUS

⅓   cup orange juice   ¼   cup maple syrup
1   Vidalia Sweet Onion   1   tablespoon butter

Put orange juice in single oven proof side dish. Peel onion and put in dish. Top with maple syrup and butter. Cover and bake 3/4 hour or until as tender as desired.

Mrs. L. P. Pleasants, Jr.
Mablehead Neck, MA

VIDALIA & APPLE DIET

1   medium Vidalia Sweet Onion   Cinnamon and/or nutmeg,
4   medium Granny Smith apples   to taste
        or Red Delicious   1   tablespoon canola or olive oil

Peel onion. Half and cut into ¼-inch diagonal slices. Core apples and cut into ¼-inch diagonal slices. Heat oil in pan. Add onions and sauté until onions begin to soften. Add apples to onions and continue to sauté over medium heat for 2 to 3 minutes, stirring frequently. Season with cinnamon and/or nutmeg. Turn fire on low. Cover and cook for 2 more minutes. Best if served immediately. Can be held on warm fire until time to serve.
Serves 4.

"Great with pork chops, ham slices, grilled chicken or Cornish game hens."

Eyvonne Jenkins
Escondido, CA

VIDALIA ONION BUTTER

10   to 12 Vidalia Sweet Onions   Spring water, to cover
     Olive, sesame or corn oil   Sea salt, pinch

In large pot with cover, sauté sliced onions in oil until transparent. Cover with water, add salt and bring to boil. Simmer for 24 hours and boil remaining off. Onions will be brownish and make a great sandwich spread.
Yields 3 to 4 cups.

"This is a basic macrobiotic recipe."

Cheryl A. Foster
Middletown, RI

VIDALIA ONIONS IN VERMOUTH

2   Vidalia Sweet Onions per   Salt, optional
        person   Pepper, optional
     Dry vermouth

Peel onions and cut a small plug out of center of each. Place in greased, deep round Pyrex baking dish. Pour ⅓ cup dry vermouth over each onion. Season to taste with salt and pepper, if desired. Bake covered at 350 degrees for approximately 1 hour or until tender.

Mrs. Rodman Townsend
Knoxville, TN

VIDALIA'S SOUTHERN SWEETIES

2	pounds medium Vidalia Sweet Onions	½	cup finely grated Parmesan cheese
2	tablespoons butter, plus butter for baking dish	1	tablespoon Worcestershire sauce
	Salt	½	cup whipping cream
	Pepper	1	teaspoon arrowroot
8	strips country bacon		Paprika
1	8-ounce package cream cheese, at room temperature		Mint leaves, fresh
8	ounces fresh mushrooms, sliced	4	thin slices Provolone cheese (optional)

Skin and quarter onions. Place in well buttered baking dish. Drizzle melted butter over onions. Season with salt and pepper to taste. Cover and bake at 350 degrees for 20 to 25 minutes or until onions begin to soften. Drain and set aside. Cut bacon into 1-inch pieces and fry until golden, not crisp. Add cream cheese and simmer until melted; blend into bacon grease. Add mushrooms; more salt and pepper to taste, and simmer 3 to 4 minutes. Pour into mixing bowl. Blend in Parmesan cheese, Worcestershire sauce, whipping cream, and arrowroot. Pour mixture over onions. Sprinkle lightly with paprika, if desired. Bake uncovered at 350 degrees for an additional 15 minutes or until cheese mixture begins to bubble. Remove casserole and garnish with fresh mint leaves. Serves 4.

Note: Optional serving suggestions. Divide baked onions into four individual serving bowls. Top with slice of Provolone cheese. Place under broiler until cheese begins to melt. Remove immediately, sprinkle lightly with paprika, if desired. Serve.

"This is real yummy!!! I was a finalist with this recipe in a local amateur chef contest."

Marilyn Basinger
Boulder City, NA
Finalist
20th Annual Amateur
Chef Competition

DINNER QUESADILLAS

6	burrito sized flour tortillas	1	large or 2 medium Vidalia Sweet Onions, thinly sliced and separated into rings
1	8-ounce jar of favorite chunky salsa, hot or medium whichever your prefer	1	teaspoon fresh cilantro per tortilla, chopped
2	boneless, skinless chicken breast halves, cooked and shredded or canned chicken pieces	8	ounces grated cheese, Jack cheese with jalapeños, plain Jack cheese or Cheddar.
1	5-ounce can chopped chili peppers, or one 5-ounce can of jalapeño peppers if you really like heat		

Heat a non-stick type griddle on stove top as if you were going to make pancakes. No oil is needed. Assemble quesadillas as follows: Cover 1 side of the tortilla with a light coating of salsa, then on ½ of the tortilla, put a 6th of the shredded chicken, a tablespoon of chilis and a generous amount of onion rings. Add a sprinkling of cilantro and a 6th of the cheese. Fold the empty half of the tortilla over the full half, making certain no filling hangs out over the edges. Place 2 filled tortillas at a time on the griddle and cook until the bottom side begins to crisp and turn brown. Flip and repeat with the other side. This whole process will take no more than 4 or 5 minutes per side over a medium heat on a pre-warmed griddle. Repeat until all quesadillas are cooked. The cheese will melt, the tortilla will cook, the filling will heat and the onions will still be crisp and crunchy. Serves 3 to 4.

"Serve with a salad, rice and beans and pass the extra salsa not used in the preparation. This is a flavorful and healthful meal, full of fiber but low in fat and cholesterol."

Carolyn Hyatt
Santa Cruz, CA

VIDALIA ONION QUESADILLAS

Vegetable cooking spray
1 teaspoon canola oil
1 large Vidalia sweet onion, coarsely chopped
1 clove garlic, minced
¼ cup chopped green bell pepper
¼ cup chopped red bell pepper

4 8-inch flour tortillas
2 ounces low fat shredded Cheddar cheese
1 tablespoon reduced calorie margarine
Sour cream
Picante sauce

Spray non-stick skillet with cooking spray and heat oil over medium heat. Add onions and caramelize by cooking over low heat, covered about 30 to 35 minutes. Add garlic and bell pepper during last 5 minutes of cooking time and increase heat to medium-low. Soften tortillas if necessary by heating in the microwave wrapped in paper towels about 15 seconds. Divide onion mixture evenly into half of each tortilla, leaving ½ border around the edge. Sprinkle each with 2 tablespoons of cheese and fold each tortilla in half to form a half moon shape. Spray skillet with more cooking spray and melt margarine over medium heat and sauté the quesadillas 2 to 3 minute on each side until golden. Garnish with sour cream and serve with picante sauce if desired.

Paula Golding
Highlands Ranch, CO

SWEET ONION PIZZA

1	pound sliced Vidalia Sweet Onions		Freshly grated Parmesan cheese
	Butter (to saute onions)	1	cup flour
4	tablespoons butter	1	tablespoon sugar
4	tablespoons flour	1	teaspoon baking powder
2	cups boiling milk		Pinch of salt
	Salt	8	tablespoons butter
	White pepper	2	eggs

Peel, slice and sauté onions in a small amount of butter. In a small sauce pan, melt 4 tablespoons butter over medium heat. When melted add flour, stirring continuously. Cook a few minutes. Before flour starts to brown, add boiling milk slowly, stirring constantly. Continue stirring and bring sauce to boil, and boil about 5 minutes until thickened. Flavor to taste with salt, white pepper and Parmesan cheese. Add to the onions and reserve. To make pastry, combine flour, sugar, baking powder, salt, 8 tablespoons butter and eggs and mix. Roll the dough into a ball, cover and refrigerate for about 10 minutes. Butter a 10-inch pie pan and spread the cooled dough into the pan, in small pieces, using your hands to stretch the dough, covering the bottom and sides of the pan. Pour sauce, then onion mixture into the dough lined pan. Bake in a medium 350 degree oven about 30 minutes or until pie edges are golden brown. Yields 8 to 10 slices.

"This recipe works well with sliced mushrooms or a combination of both Vidalia Sweet Onions and mushrooms."

Anthony M. Santare
Alameda, CA

WHITE PIZZA

12	inch round prepared pizza dough		Pepper, cracked to taste
¼	to ½ cup olive oil	1	tablespoon rosemary, dried
2	large Vidalia Sweet Onions Salt, pinch	1½	cups shredded Mozzarella cheese

Roll dough to pan size. Use 2 tablespoons olive oil to spread on pizza pan. Place pizza dough on pan. Add 2 large Vidalia sweet onions sliced very thin and arranged on top of dough. Sprinkle remaining oil evenly over onions. Add salt, cracked pepper and rosemary evenly over onions. Next, sprinkle the cheese on top. Bake in 425 to 450 degree oven for 15 to 20 minutes. Yields one 12-inch pizza. Serves 4 to 6.

"One cup sliced black olives may be added if desired. Never a failure with a Vidalia."

Barbara St. Onge
Haverhill, MA

Indexes

By Category

Alphabetically

By Contributor

BLAND FARMS

Index By Category

APPETIZERS & HORS D'OEUVRES

Arms Roll Ups _____ 10
Bert's Zesty Vidalia Onion Dip _____ 10
Cassie's Vidalia Cracker Appetizer _____ 11
Cocktail Dip Guacamole _____ 11
Deviled Vidalia Sweet Onions _____ 12
Fried Vidalia Sweet Onion Rings _____ 12
Hors D'oeuvre _____ 13
Hors D'oeuvre for Cocktails _____ 13
Microwaved Vidalia Sweet Onions _____ 14
Strohm Vidalia Sweet Onion Rings _____ 15
Vidalia Sweet Onion and Cheese Dip _____ 17
Vidalia Sweet Onion Appetizer _____ 16
Vidalia Sweet Onion Appetizer Squares _____ 14
Vidalia Sweet Onion Hors D'oeuvre _____ 16
Vidalia Sweet Onion Hors D'oeuvres _____ 18
Vidalia Sweet Onion Surprise _____ 16
Vidalia Sweet Onion Tarts _____ 15
Vidalia Sweet Onion Wedgies _____ 18
Vidalia Sweet Onion with
 Creamy Olive Dip Appetizer _____ 17

BAKED & STUFFED TREATS

Amendment to "Bland Family Favorite" ___ 64
Baked Onions A La Mode _____ 64
Baked Onions with Herb Butter _____ 65
Baked Vidalia Onion _____ 65
Baked Vidalia Sweets _____ 68
Baked Vidalia with Brown Sugar _____ 67
Baked Vidalias and Peanuts _____ 67
Baked Vidalias with Parmesan _____ 68
Baked Vidalias with Swiss Cheese _____ 68
Baked Vidalia Sweet Onions with Rice _____ 66
Bette's Baked Onions-French Style _____ 69
Big Baked Onions _____ 69
Baked Vidalia Sweet Onions _____ 66
Creamed Vidalia Onions _____ 70
Honey Baked Vidalias _____ 70
Jane's Baked Onions _____ 71
Judith's Baked Onions _____ 71
June's Sweet Onions _____ 72
Martha's Baked Vidalia Onions _____ 72
Onions Calabrese (Italy) _____ 73
Onions Stuffed with Sausage _____ 75
Simply Baked Sweet Vidalia _____ 73
Stuffed Baked Onions _____ 76

Stuffed Onion Rolls _____ 77
Stuffed Onions _____ 76
Stuffed Peppers _____ 78
Stuffed Vidalia Onions _____ 78
Sweet & Sour Onions _____ 74
The Tease Of Spring _____ 74
Vidalia Onion & Tomato Bake _____ 75
Vidalia Sweet Onion Bake _____ 72

BREADS & LOAVES

Broccoli Cornbread _____ 20
Three Grain Filled Vidalia
 Sweet Onion Rings _____ 21
Vidalia Sweet Onion Ring Loaf _____ 20
Vidalia Sweet Onion Upside Down Bread ___ 21

CASSEROLES & SOUFFLEES

Baked Cabbage Lasagna _____ 80
Baked Onion Casserole _____ 81
Baked Rice & Mushroom Casserole _____ 81
Broccoli & Onion Casserole _____ 83
Broccoli, Corn, Onion Casserole _____ 82
Carrot-Onion Casserole _____ 83
Cebola Casserole _____ 84
Cheesy Ham'n Bean Casserole _____ 84
Cheryl's Vidalia Onion Casserole _____ 85
Chicken & Vidalia Onion Casserole _____ 85
Corn Casserole _____ 86
Dixie's Vidalia Casserole _____ 86
Easy Casserole _____ 87
Ethel's Vidalia Onion Casserole _____ 87
Georgia Casserole _____ 88
Gladys' Casserole _____ 88
Grandma Henny's Casserole _____ 89
Hawaiian Onions _____ 89
Heavenly Vidalias _____ 90
Honeyed Onions _____ 90
Italian Sausage, Onions & Potato Casserole _ 91
Jody's Vidalia Onion Casserole _____ 91
Layered Vidalia Sweet Onion Casserole _____ 92
Lip-Smacking Vidalia Sweet Onion Casserole 92
Onion & Dill Casserole _____ 96
Onion & Potato Casserole _____ 95
Onion Casserole _____ 93
Onion Casserole A La Toma _____ 94
Onion Casserole with Cayenne _____ 94
Onion Casserole with Cornbread Stuffing ___ 93

Onion Celeste _____ 95
Onion Cheese Casserole _____ 96
Onion-Tuna-Potato Casserole _____ 97
Sausage & Rice Casserole _____ 98
Savory Vidalia Onions _____ 97
Soubise _____ 98
Soubise with Cheese _____ 99
Summer Casserole _____ 99
Sweet & Sour Vidalias _____ 100
Vidaia Onion Casserole _____ 101
Vidalia Onion Cheese Strata _____ 102
Vidalia Onion Pudding _____ 102
Vidalia Onion Souffle _____ 103
Vidalia Onion/Cheese Casserole _____ 101
Vidalia Onions Amadine _____ 100
Vidalia Sweet Onion Casserole _____ 103
Vidalia Sweet Onion Souffle _____ 104
Whole Vidalias with Sweet Pea Dressing
    (Cover Recipe) _____ 82

MEATS CHICKEN & SEAFOOD

Baked Pork Chops with Vidalias _____ 138
Barbecued Hamburgers _____ 128
Burger Stuffed Vidalias _____ 128
Chicken & Onions _____ 132
Chicken Pockets with Vidalia Yogurt Sauce 133
Chicken Skillet Stew _____ 133
Chinese Beef with Vidalia Sweet Onions ___ 129
Curried Chicken _____ 134
Curried Shrimp _____ 141
Gourmet Chicken Liver Saute-Ole _____ 134
Hawaiian Chicken _____ 135
Kit's Roast Pork for Onion Lovers _____ 139
Lamb Stuffed Vidalias _____ 136
Liver & Vidalia Onions _____ 137
Liver Onion Delight _____ 137
Onion & Shrimp Creole _____ 141
Pan Fried Orange Roughy _____ 142
Pennsylvania Dutch Beef Onon Stew _____ 130
Pork Chop with Pineapple _____ 138
Sausage Dressing _____ 140
Scrambled Eggs with Onions
    & Smoked Salmon _____ 142
Sergio's White Chicken _____ 135
Sherried Beef-Onion Bake _____ 130
Special Chicken & Onions _____ 136
Steak Vidalia _____ 131
Tex-Mex Steak & Onions _____ 131
Tuna Stuffed Onions _____ 143
Vidalia Guacamole _____ 132
Vidalia Onion & Tuna _____ 143
Vidalia Onion Salsa with
    Pork Tenderloin Strips _____ 139
Vidalia Sweet Onion Chile Con Carne _____ 129

PICKLES, RELISHES & SAUCES

Baked Onion/Apple Relish _____ 166
Blue Cheese & Onions _____ 160
Diane's Marinated Onions _____ 161
Dilled Cucumbers & Onions _____ 160
Dilly Onion Rings _____ 160
Dutch Cucumber & Onions _____ 161
Hot Vidalia Sweet Onion Dipping Sauce ___ 169
Lena's Pickled Onions _____ 164
Lori's Marinated Onions _____ 162
Marinated Cucumber & Vidalia Sweet Onions 162
Marinated Vidalia Onions _____ 162
Marinated Vidalia Sweet Onions _____ 163
Onion & Mushroom Wine Sauce _____ 170
Onion Relish _____ 166
Onion-Lemon Chutney _____ 165
Onions in Mustard Sauce _____ 170
Peggy's Marinated Onions _____ 163
Refrigerator Cukes & Onions _____ 164
Vidalia Sweet Onion Parmesan Relish _____ 167
Vidalia Sweet Onion Relish _____ 167
Vidalia Sweet Onion Sauce _____ 169
Vidalia Sweet Onions in Dill Sauce _____ 168
Zesty Onion-Corn Relish _____ 168

PIES QUICHE & OMELET

Albert's Vidalia sweet Onion Pie _____ 146
Bev's Vidalia Onion Pie _____ 147
Blue Cheese & Onion Tart _____ 158
Carolyn's Vidalia Sweet Onion Pie _____ 146
Catherine's Onion Pie _____ 148
Chili Pepper-Vidalia Onion Quiche _____ 156
Cindy's Sunday Pie (For Tired Gardeners!)_ 149
Company Cheese & Onion Pie _____ 148
Delicious Vidalia Sweet Onion Pie _____ 149
Edna's Vidalia Sweet Onion Pie _____ 150
Georgia Onion Pie _____ 151
Omelet For Dieters _____ 155
Onion & Cheese Quiche _____ 157
Ruth's Onion Pie _____ 150
Skilligalee Onion Pie _____ 152
Supper Omelet For Two _____ 155
Vidalia Onion Pie By Drew _____ 153
Vidalia Onion Quiche _____ 156
Vidalia Sweet Onion Pie _____ 152
Vidalia Sweet Onion Pie
    With Parmesan Cheese _____ 153
Zucchini & Onion Pie _____ 154
Zwiebel Kuchen (Onion Pie) _____ 154

SALADS &
SALAD DRESSINGS

Beverly's Orange-Vidalia Sweet Onion Salad 24
Casual California Salad 24
Colorado Macaroni Salad 25
Corn, Tomato & Vidalia Sweet Onion Salad 25
Cornbread Salad 26
Country Club Vidalia Sweet Onions 26
Crunchy, Cold Pea Salad 27
Deluxe Thousand Island Dressing 42
Diabetic, Lo-Cal, Dietary Snack or Meal 27
English Summer Salad 28
German Potato Salad 28
Italian Salad 29
Italian-Pasta-Vidalia Sweet Onion Salad 29
Kidney Bean Soup 30
Marinated Vidalia Sweet Onion & Mixed
   Vegetable Salad 31
Mustard Onion Dressing 42
My Husband's Favorite Carrot Salad 31
Orange & Onion Salad 34
Potato Salad 30
Ron's Simple & Delicious Peppers 32
Sauteed Onions/Hearts of Celery with a Twist 32
Scandinavian Salad 33
Some Kinda Salad 33
Tomato and Onion Salad 35
Tomato Salad 34
Tuna Salad 35
Vidalia Onion & Cucumber Toss 37
Vidalia Onion & Tomato Salad 39
Vidalia Onion Salad 38
Vidalia Onions & Tomatoes 39
Vidalia Onions with Balsamic Vinegar 36
Vidalia Revelry 40
Vidalia Sweet Onion Salad 40
Vidalia Sweet Onion Salad Dressing 43
Vidalia Sweet Onion Salad Supreme 38
Vidalia Vinegar 43
Vidalia-Beef Vinaigrette 36
Vidaliaz Coleslaw with Capers 37
Vine La Vidalia Salade 41
White Bean, Caper & Onion Salad 41

SOUPS & SANDWICHES

"Babywiches" 55
Basil, Onion & Tomato Sandwich (BOT) 56
Best Onion Soup 46
Cold Cream of Vidalia Onion Soup 47
Corn Chowder 46
Cream of Onion, Potato, Cheese Soup 48
Cream of Sweet Onion & Sauterne Soup 48
Cream of Vidalia Onion Soup 49

Fork & Knife Onion Soup 50
French Onion Soup I 50
French Onion Soup II (The Very Best) 51
French Onion Soup III 51
Grilled Vidalia-Pineapple Sandwich 56
Hot Dogs & Onions 57
Italian Onion & Bread Soup 52
Monique's French Onion Soup 53
Old Fashioned Onion Sandwich 57
Onion & Red Pepper Soup 53
Onion Pocket Sandwich 58
Onion Soup Au Gratin 52
Open-Faced Vidalia Sweet Onion Peanut Butter
Sandwich 58
Orange/Onion Sandwich 57
Peanut Butter & Onion Sandwich 59
Super Onion Sandwich 60
Tuna Sandwiches or Salad 60
Vidalia Onion Rivel Soup 54
Vidalia Onion Sandwich 61
Vidalia Onion Soup 55
Vidalia Sweet Onion & Mushroom Soup 54
Vidalia Sweet Onion Grilled Sandwich 62
Vidalia/Scali Onion Sandwich 61

SPECIAL VIDALIA SWEET
ONION TREATS

Barbeque Onions 172
Barbeque Side Dish 172
Caramelized Vidalia Sweet Onions
   Over Pasta 173
Chrysanthemum Onions 173
Creamy Chili Sauce 183
Dinner Quesadillas 187
Great Grilled Vidalia Sweet Onions 174
Grilled Onions 175
Grilled Vidalia Sweet Onions 174
Microwave Vidalia Sweet Onions 175
Nancy's Bourbon Onions 176
Party Ratatouille 176
Sauteed Onions with Catsup 178
Sauteed Onions with Orzo 179
Sauteed Vidalia Onions 179
Sauteed Vidalia Sweet Onions
   and Mushrooms 178
Savory Vidalia Sweet Onion Turnovers 177
Seasoned Flour 183
Sherried Gourmet Onions 180
Sherry Glazed Vidlia Onions 180
Steamed Vidalia "Pee Wees" in Sweet White
Sauce 181
Sweet Onion Pizza 189
Tamale Sandwich with Vidalia Sweet Onions 182
The Quickie 177

The Ultimate Onion _____ 182
Uncle Bob's Enhanced Vidalias _____ 183
Vidalia's Southern Sweeties _____ 186
Vidalia & Apple Diet _____ 184
Vidalia Delicious _____ 184
Vidalia Onion Butter _____ 185
Vidalia Onion Quesadillas _____ 188
Vidalia Onions in Vermouth _____ 185
White Pizza _____ 190

VEGETABLES & STIR FRIES

Baked Corn-Cheesy Onion _____ 106
Baked Potatoes Delight _____ 117
Baked Potatoes Supreme _____ 118
Braised Onions _____ 110
Caramelized Vidalia Onions Over Pasta ___ 110
Cheese-Scalloped Onions _____ 111
Chicken & Vegetable Stir-Fry _____ 125
Country Cabbage _____ 107
Creamed Chunky Spinach _____ 122
Delicious Potatoes _____ 118
Green Beans Provencale _____ 108
Green Beans with Tomato Sauce _____ 108
Green Vegetable Pie _____ 123
Greens & Beans _____ 107

Mabel's Paprika Onions _____ 111
Marinated Carrots _____ 106
Mom's Green Bean Dish _____ 109
Noodle Onion Kugel (Pudding) _____ 109
Not So Plain Potatoes _____ 119
Onion Parmesan _____ 112
Potato Pudding _____ 119
Saucy Vidalias Italiano _____ 112
Side Dish Vidalias _____ 113
Spanish Rice _____ 121
Steamed Fresh Vegetable Mix _____ 124
Stir-Fry Liver & Onions _____ 126
Summer Squash Parmesan _____ 122
Susie's Bland Farms Vidalia Sweet Onions
    & Potatoes _____ 113
Sweet Onion Potato Cakes _____ 120
Sweet Onion Potatoes _____ 120
Sweet Vidalia Onions & Mustard Greens ___ 114
Sweet Vidalia Stir-Fry _____ 126
Twice-Baked Squash Boats _____ 123
Vegetable Casserole _____ 124
Vegetarian Indian Corn & Rice _____ 125
Veggie Vidalia _____ 114
Vidalia & Bacon Veggie _____ 115
Vidalia Onion Augratin _____ 116
Vidalia Onion Shortcake _____ 116
Vidalia Onions & Sweet red Peppers Ishmael 117
Vidalia Scalloped Potatoes _____ 121
Vidalias A La Gorgonzola _____ 115

Alphabetical Index

A

Albert's Vidalia Sweet Onion Pie _____ 146
Amendment to
    "Bland Family Favorite" _____ 64
Arms Roll Ups _____ 10

B

Babywiches _____ 55
Baked Cabbage Lasagna ___ _____ 80
Baked Corn-Cheesy Onion _____ 106
Baked Onion A La Mode _____ 64
Baked Onion Casserole _____ 81
Baked Onion with Herb Butter _____ 65
Baked Onion/Apples Relish _____ 166
Baked Pork Chops with Vidalias _____ 138
Baked Potatoes Delight _____ 117
Baked Potatoes Supreme _____ 118
Baked Rice and Mushroom Casserole _____ 81
Baked Vidalia Onion _____ 65
Baked Vidalia Sweet Onions _____ 66
Baked Vidalia Sweet Onions with Rice _____ 66
Baked Vidalia Sweets _____ 68
Baked Vidalias with Brown Sugar _____ 67
Baked Vidalias with Parmesan _____ 68
Baked Vidalias with Peanuts _____ 67
Baked Vidalias with Swiss Cheese _____ 68
Barbecue Onions _____ 172
Barbecue Side Dish _____ 172
Barbecued Hamburgers _____ 128
Basil, Onion and Tomato Sandwich (BOT) _ 56
Bert's Zesty Vidalia Onion Dip _____ 10
Best Ever Onion Casserole _____ 82
Best Onion Soup _____ 46
Bette's Baked Onions-French Style _____ 69
Bev's Vidalia Onion Pie _____ 147
Beverly's Orange-Vidalia
    Sweet Onion Salad _____ 24
Big Baked Onions _____ 69
Blue Cheese and Onion _____ 160
Blue Cheese and Onion Tart _____ 158
Braised Onions _____ 110
Broccoli and Onion Casserole _____ 83
Broccoli Cornbread _____ 20
Broccoli, Corn and Onion Casserole _____ 82
Burger Stuffed Vidalias _____ 128

C

Caramelized Vidalia Onions
    Over Pasta _____ 110
Caramelized Vidalia Sweet Onions
    Over Pasta _____ 173
Carolyn's Vidalia Sweet Onion Pie_____ 146
Carrot-Onion Casserole _____ 83
Cassie's Vidalia Cracker Appetizer_____ 11
Casual California Salad _____ 24
Catherine's Onion Pie _____ 148
Cebola Casserole _____ 84
Cheese-Scalloped Onions _____ 111
Cheesy Ham'n Bean Casserole_____ 84
Cheryl's Vidalia Onion Casserole _____ 85
Chicken and Onions _____ 132
Chicken and Vegetable Stir-Fry _____ 125
Chicken and Vidalia Onion Casserole _____ 85
Chicken Pockets with
    Vidalia Yogurt Sauce _____ 133
Chicken Skillet Stew _____ 133
Chili Pepper-Vidalia Sweet Onion Quiche _ 156
Chinese Beef with Vidalia Sweet Onions ___ 129
Chrysanthemum Onions _____ 173
Cindy's Sunday Pie
    (For Tired Gardeners!) _____ 149
Cocktail Dip Guacamole _____ 11
Cold Cream of Vidalia Onion Soup _____ 47
Colorado Macaroni Salad _____ 25
Company Cheese and Onion Pie _____ 148
Corn Casserole_____ 86
Corn Chowder _____ 46
Corn, Tomato &
    Vidalia Sweet Onion Salad _____ 25
Cornbread Salad _____ 26
Country Cabbage _____ 107
Country Club Vidalia Sweet Onions _____ 26
Cream of Onion, Potato
    & Cheese Soup _____ 47
Cream of Sweet Onion and
    Sauterne Soup _____ 48
Cream of Vidalia Onion Soup _____ 49
Creamed Chunky Spinach_____ 122
Creamed Vidalia Onions _____ 70
Creamy Chili Sauce _____ 183
Crunchy, Cold Pea Salad _____ 27
Curried Chicken _____ 134
Curried Shrimp_____ 141

D

Delicious Potatoes — 118
Delicious Vidalia Sweet Onion Pie — 149
Deluxe Thousand Island Dressing — 42
Deviled Vidalia Sweet Onions — 12
Diabetic, Lo-Cal, Dietary Snack or Meal — 27
Diane's Marinated Onions — 161
Dilled Cucumbers and Onions — 161
Dilly Onion Rings — 160
Dinner Quesadillas — 187
Dixie's Vidalia Casserole — 86

E

Easy Casserole — 87
Edna's Vidalia Sweet Onion Pie — 150
English Summer Salad — 28
Ethel's Vidalia Onion Casserole — 87

F

Fork and Knife Onion Soup — 50
French Onion Soup I — 50
French Onion Soup II (The Very Best) — 51
French Onion Soup III — 51
Fried Vidalia Sweet Onion Rings — 12

G

Georgia Casserole — 88
Georgia Onion Pie — 151
German Potato Salad — 28
Gladys' Casserole — 88
Gourmet Chicken Liver Saute-Ole — 134
Grandma Henny's Casserole — 89
Great Grilled Vidalia Sweet Onions — 174
Green Beans Provencale — 108
Green Beans with Tomato Sauce — 108
Green Vegetable Pie — 123
Greens and Beans — 107
Grilled Onions — 175
Grilled Vidalia Sweet Onions — 174
Grilled Vidalia-Pineapple Sandwich — 56

H

Hawaiian Chicken — 135
Hawaiian Onions — 89
Heavenly Vidalias — 90
Honey Baked Vidalias — 70
Honeyed Onions — 90
Hors D'oeuvre — 13
Hors D'oeuvre for Cocktails — 13
Hot Dogs and Onions — 57
Hot Vidalia Sweet Onion Dipping Sauce — 169

I

Italian Onion and Bread Soup — 52
Italian Salad — 29
Italian Sausage, Onions & Potato Casserole — 91
Italian-Pasta-Vidalia Sweet Onion Salad — 29

J

Jane's Baked Onions — 71
Jody's Vidalia Onion Casserole — 91
Judith's Baked Onions — 71
June's Sweet Onions — 72

K

Kidney Bean Soup — 30
Kit's Roast Pork for Onion Lovers — 139

L

Lamb Stuffed Vidalias — 136
Layered Vidalia Sweet Onion Casserole — 92
Lena's Pickled Onions — 164
Lip-Smacking Vidalia Sweet Onion Casserole — 92
Liver and Vidalia Onions — 137
Liver Onion Delight — 137
Lori's Marinated Onions — 162

M

Mabel's Paprika Onions _____ 111
Marinated Carrots _____ 106
Marinated Cucumber and
   Vidalia Sweet Onions _____ 162
Marinated Vidalia Onions _____ 162
Marinated Vidalia Sweet Onion and Mix
   Vegetable Salad _____ 31
Marinated Vidalia Sweet Onions _____ 163
Martha's Baked Vidalia Onions _____ 72
Microwave Vidalia Sweet Onions _____ 175
Microwave Vidalia Sweet Onions _____ 14
Mom's Green Bean Dish _____ 109
Monique's French Onion Soup _____ 53
Mustard Onion Dressing _____ 42
My Husband's Favorite Carrot Salad _____ 31

N

Nancy's Bourbon Onions _____ 176
Noodle Onion Kugel (Pudding) _____ 109
Not So Plain Potatoes _____ 119

O

Old Fashioned Onion Sandwich _____ 57
Omelet For Dieters _____ 155
Onion and Cheese Quiche _____ 157
Onion and Dill Casserole _____ 96
Onion and Mushroom Wine Sauce _____ 170
Onion and Potato Casserole _____ 95
Onion and Red Pepper Soup _____ 53
Onion and Shrimp Creole _____ 141
Onion Au Gratin _____ 52
Onion Casserole _____ 93
Onion Casserole A La Toma _____ 94
Onion Casserole with Cayenne _____ 94
Onion Casserole with Cornbread Stuffing ___ 93
Onion Celeste _____ 95
Onion Cheese Casserole _____ 96
Onion Parmesan _____ 112
Onion Pocket Sandwich _____ 58
Onion Relish _____ 166
Onion-Lemon Chutney _____ 165
Onion-Tuna-Potato Casserole _____ 97

Onions Calabrese (Italy) _____ 73
Onions in Mustard Sauce _____ 170
Onions Stuffed with Sausage _____ 75
Open-Faced Vidalia Sweet Onion &
   Peanut Butter Sandwich _____ 58
Orange and Onion Salad _____ 34
Orange-Onion Sandwich _____ 57

P

Pan Fried Orange Roughy _____ 142
Party Ratatouille _____ 176
Peanut Butter and Onion Sandwich _____ 59
Peggy's Marinated Onions _____ 163
Pennsylvania Dutch Beef Onion Stew ___ 130
Pork Chops with Pineapple _____ 138
Potato Pudding _____ 119
Potato Salad _____ 30

Q

Quickie _____ 177

R

Refrigerator Cukes and Onions _____ 164
Ron's Simple and Delicious Peppers _____ 32
Ruth's Onion Pie _____ 150

S

Saucy Vidalias Italiano _____ 112
Sausage and Rice Casserole _____ 98
Sausage Dressing _____ 140
Sautéed Onions with Catsup _____ 178
Sautéed Onions/Hearts of Celery
   with a Twist _____ 32
Sautéed Vidalia Onions _____ 179
Sautéed Vidalia Onions with Orzo _____ 179
Sautéed Vidalia Sweet Onions
   and Mushrooms _____ 178
Savory Vidalia Onions _____ 97
Savory Vidalia Sweet Onion Turnovers ___ 177

Scandinavian Salad _____ 33
Scrambled Eggs with Onions and
    Smoked Salmon _____ 142
Seasoned Flour _____ 183
Sergio's White Chicken _____ 135
Sherried Beef-Onion Bake _____ 130
Sherried Gourmet Onions _____ 180
Sherry Glazed Vidalia Onions _____ 180
Side Dish Vidalias _____ 113
Simply Baked Sweet Vidalia _____ 73
Skilligalee Onion Pie _____ 152
Some Kinda Salad _____ 33
Soubise _____ 98
Soubise with Cheese _____ 99
Special Chicken and Onions _____ 136
Steak Vidalia _____ 131
Steamed Fresh Vegetable Mix _____ 124
Steamed Vidalia "Pee Wees"
    in Sweet White Sauce _____ 181
Stir-Fry Liver and Onions _____ 126
Strohm Vidalia Sweet Onion Rings _____ 15
Stuffed Baked Onions _____ 76
Stuffed Onion Rolls _____ 77
Stuffed Onions _____ 76
Stuffed Peppers _____ 78
Stuffed Vidalia Onions _____ 78
Summer Casserole _____ 99
Summer Squash Parmesan _____ 122
Super Omelet For Two _____ 155
Super Onion Sandwich _____ 60
Susie's Bland Farms Vidalia Sweet Onion
    and Potatoes _____ 113
Sweet and Sour Onions _____ 74
Sweet and Sour Vidalias _____ 100
Sweet Onion Pizza _____ 189
Sweet Onion Potato Cakes _____ 120
Sweet Onion Potatoes _____ 120
Sweet Vidalia Onions and
    Mustard Greens _____ 114
Sweet Vidalia Stir-Fry _____ 126

T

Tamale Sandwich with
    Vidalia Sweet Onions _____ 182
Tease of Spring _____ 74
Tex-Mex Steak and Onions _____ 131
Three Grain Filled
    Vidalia Sweet Onion Rings _____ 21

Tomato and Onion Salad _____ 35
Tomato Salad _____ 34
Tuna Salad _____ 35
Tuna Sandwiches or Salad _____ 60
Tuna Stuffed Onions _____ 143
Twice-Baked Squash Boats _____ 123

U

Ultimate Onion _____ 182
Uncle Bob's Enhanced Vidalias _____ 183

V

Vegetable Casserole _____ 124
Vegetarian Indian Corn and Rice _____ 125
Veggie Vidalia _____ 114
Vidalia Onion Soufflé _____ 104
Vidalia's Southern Sweeties _____ 186
Vidalia and Apple Diet _____ 184
Vidalia and Bacon Veggie _____ 115
Vidalia Coleslaw with Capers _____ 37
Vidalia Delicious _____ 184
Vidalia Guacamole _____ 132
Vidalia Onion and Cucumber Toss _____ 37
Vidalia Onion and Tomato Bake _____ 75
Vidalia Onion and Tomato Salad _____ 39
Vidalia Onion and Tuna _____ 143
Vidalia Onion Au Gratin _____ 116
Vidalia Onion Butter _____ 185
Vidalia Onion Casserole _____ 101
Vidalia Onion Cheese Strata _____ 102
Vidalia Onion Pie By Drew _____ 153
Vidalia Onion Pudding _____ 102
Vidalia Onion Quesadillas _____ 188
Vidalia Onion quiche _____ 156
Vidalia Onion Rivel Soup _____ 54
Vidalia Onion Salsa with
    Pork Tenderloin Strips _____ 139
Vidalia Onion Sandwich _____ 61
Vidalia Onion Shortcake _____ 116
Vidalia Onion Soup _____ 55
Vidalia Onion/Cheese Casserole _____ 101
Vidalia Onions Amadine _____ 100
Vidalia Onions and
    Sweet Red Peppers Ishmael _____ 117
Vidalia Onions and Tomatoes _____ 39

Vidalia Onions in Vermouth _____ 185
Vidalia Onion Salad _____ 38
Vidalia Onions with Balsamic Vinegar _____ 36
Vidalia Reverly _____ 40
Vidalia Scalloped Potatoes _____ 121
Vidalia Sweet Onion and Cheese Dip _____ 17
Vidalia Sweet Onion and Mushroom Soup _____ 54
Vidalia Sweet Onion Appetizer _____ 16
Vidalia Sweet Onion Appetizer Squares _____ 14
Vidalia Sweet Onion Bake _____ 72
Vidalia Sweet Onion Casserole _____ 103
Vidalia Sweet Onion Chile Con Carne _____ 129
Vidalia Sweet Onion Grilled Sandwich _____ 62
Vidalia Sweet Onion Hors D'oeuvre _____ 16
Vidalia Sweet Onion Hors D'oeuvre _____ 18
Vidalia Sweet Onion Parmesan Relish _____ 167
Vidalia Sweet Onion Pie _____ 152
Vidalia Sweet Onion Pie
   with Parmesan Cheese _____ 153
Vidalia Sweet Onion Relish _____ 167
Vidalia Sweet Onion Ring Loaf _____ 20
Vidalia Sweet Onion Salad _____ 40
Vidalia Sweet Onion Salad Dressing _____ 43
Vidalia Sweet Onion Salad Supreme _____ 38
Vidalia Sweet Onion Sauce _____ 169
Vidalia Sweet Onion Soufflé _____ 104
Vidalia Sweet Onion Surprise _____ 16

Vidalia Sweet Onion Tarts _____ 15
Vidalia Sweet Onion Upside Down Bread _____ 21
Vidalia Sweet Onion Wedgies _____ 18
Vidalia Sweet Onion with
   Creamy Olive Dip Appetizer _____ 17
Vidalia Sweet Onions in Dill Sauce _____ 168
Vidalia Vinegar _____ 43
Vidalia-Beef Vinaigrette _____ 36
Vidalia/Scali Onion Sandwich _____ 61
Vidalias A La Gorgonzola _____ 115
Vine La Vidalia Salade _____ 41
Visalia (Vidalia) Casserole _____ 140

W

White Bean, Caper and Onion Salad _____ 41
White Pizza _____ 190

Z

Zesty Onion-Corn Relish _____ 168
Zucchini and Onion Pie _____ 154
Zwiebel Kuchen (Onion Pie) _____ 154

Contributors Index

A

Ackerman, Juanita
   Golden Bridge, NY _____ 41
Adams, Don
   Zachary, LA _____ 140
Anderson, Edna
   Sidney, NE _____ 12
Anderson, Lucille
   Newburt Park, CA _____ 57
Andis, Desi L.
   San Jose, CA _____ 162
Andree, Marie K.
   Rio Rancho, NM _____ 60
Andrews, Jacqueline D.
   Lakeland, FL _____ 149
Arms, Norma
   Allegan, MI _____ 10
Arnold, Margert E.
   Fredericksburg, VA _____ 101
Atkins, Betty
   Birmingham, MI _____ 130
Atkinsin, Paul
   Indianapolis, IN _____ 136

Augustine, Mrs. Frankie
   Glenwood Springs, CO _____ 60

B

Baker, Mary T.
   Jacksonville, AL _____ 43
Balke, Betty
   Sequim, WA _____ 106
Ballard, Joan M.
   Pacheco, CA _____ 54
Barnes, Dorothy S.
   Albuquerque NM _____ 14
Barrett, Nina
   Grandview, MO _____ 178
Barringer, Mrs. C. Minor
   Chadds Ford, PA _____ 98
Basinger, Marilyn
   Boulder City, NA _____ 186
Bater, Beverly Stewart
   Hyannis, MA _____ 90
Beale, Martha P.
   Norfolk, VA _____ 68

Belt, Eleanore A.
Chicago Heights, IL _____ 182
Berg, Mrs. John E.
Flossmoor, IL _____ 160
Bergelt, Phil
St. Cloud, FL _____ 38
Berger, Cindy
Chester Springs, PA _____ 130
Berger, Jeff
Springfield, MO _____ 64
Bernheimer, Roz & daughters
Waban, MA _____ 174
Bieda, Margaret
Oconto Falls, WI _____ 40
Bienvenu, John B.
St. Martinville, LA _____ 20
Block, Marilyn
Bethesda, MD _____ 168
Bloomberg, Jonathan
New York, NY _____ 39
Bone, Jane
Cape Coral, FL _____ 50
Borschuk, Linda
Phoenix, Az _____ 68
Boutilier, Carl W.
Block Island, RI _____ 84
Boyd, Mrs. Virgil E.
W. Sedona, AZ _____ 106
Boyer, Melinda
Atlanta, GA _____ 123
Boynton, Mrs. John
Mequan, WI _____ 179
Bozeman, Mrs. D. W.
Pecos, TX _____ 103
Brewer, W. C. Jr.
Baltimore, MD _____ 73
Brod, Ellen L.
Worcester, MA _____ 152
Brooks, Mrs. Deborah
Charlotte, NC _____ 66
Broussard, Flo
Arlington, VA _____ 58
Brown, James L.
Indianapolis, IN _____ 38
Brown, Mrs. A. C. Jr.
Norht Kingston, RI _____ 46
Buckner, Ellen
Chattanooga, TN _____ 147
Burgess, Susan C.
Georgetown, DE _____ 36
Butman, Elinor
Temple Hills, MD _____ 92
Byer, Eleanor J.
Pittsburgh, PA _____ 129

C

Cameron, Patt
Claremore, OK _____ 102
Campbell, Virginia F.
Selden, NY _____ 37
Cardy, Lettie C.
Normandy, TN _____ 148
Carver, Betty. J.
Warner Robins, GA _____ 77
Cary, Jean
Pearl River, NY _____ 178
Cekander, Joyce
Olympia Fields, IL _____ 16
Cervetti, Sergio
Brooklyn, NY _____ 135
Cheeseman, Alice
Unity, ME _____ 96
Cloeman, Noni
Knoxville, TN _____ 113
Cole, Jeane
Pioneer, CA _____ 110
Cole, Kathleen H.
Boonton Township, NJ _____ 139
Cole, Mrs. Marlin F.
Paradise Valley, AZ _____ 66
Coleman, Ruth
Orlando, FL _____ 85, 91
Colton, Joyce DiBeneddeto
Miami,FL _____ 134, 141
Cover, Barbara
Alexandria, VA _____ 102
Cumps, Marian
Sun Lakes, AZ _____ 93

D

Dahmer, Lena
Nevada, MO _____ 164
Davis, Susie
Franktown, CO _____ 113
DeFore, Carla
Bryon, GA _____ 139, 177
DeRosear, Peggy
Hamilton, IL _____ 163
Doeringer, Betty Z.
Plainfield, NJ _____ 152
Dot at Braswells
Statesboro, GA _____ 67
Dougherty, Dr. John J.
Prescott, AZ _____ 27
Drew, Leon & Mary
Laughlin, NV _____ 153
Drislane, Dennis J.
Lynnfield, MA _____ 120

E

Edwards, Mrs. E. R.
Ft. Worth, TX _____ 137
Elrod, Donald S.
Pebble Beach, CA _____ 47
English, Eugenia
Dallas, TX _____ 137
Entrikin, Lorraine
North Wales, PA _____ 49
Evenson, Violette B.
Pepperell, MA _____ 138
Evered, Jim
Denton, TX _____ 51
Ewen, Edna
Lubbock, TX _____ 81

F

Faraca, Marie
Spokane, WA _____ 29
Federighi, Francis
Schenectady, NY _____ 56
Feicht, James A.
Kittanning, PA _____ 57
Finkle, Carolyn J.
Lubbock, TX _____ 146
Fishman, Linda
Christiana, PA _____ 132
Flanigan, Vera
Camp Hill, PA _____ 42
Ford, Betsey L.
Port Hueneme, CA _____ 25
Fortino, Ruth S.
Bethlehem, PA _____ 150
Foster, Cheryl A.
Middletown, RI _____ 185

G

Gajewski, Annetta
Bridsboro, PA _____ 18
Garlick, Marguerite F.
Bowie, MD _____ 62
Geraty, Marilyn
Sacramento, CA _____ 32, 169
Gill, Cassie
Birmingham, MI _____ 11
Glass, Janie
Iowa Park, TX _____ 150
Glatthar, Cathy
King William, VA _____ 152
Gnoli, Nancy
Hartford, CT _____ 73
Golas, Mrs. Joseph
Enfield, CT _____ 58
Golding, Paula
Highlands Ranch, CO _____ 68

Gonzales, Theresa A.
Tampa, FL _____ 125
Gordaon, Joseph
New York, NY _____ 142
Gorman, Jane
Ambler, PA _____ 71
Grace-George Alexander-Greene
New York City, NY _____ 120
Graham, Laura
Lansing, MI _____ 180
Gregary, Ada Z.
Prescott, AZ _____ 131
Guarino, Joseph
Trenton, NJ _____ 115
Guidry, Mimi
Scott, LA _____ 81
Gundrey, Frances C.
Santa Fe, CA _____ 99

H

Hagopian, Diane
Waukegan, IL _____ 161
Hall, Fran
Butler, MO _____ 89
Halliday, Bob & Gloria
Potsdam, NY _____ 34
Hamker, Wava
Perrysburgh, OH _____ 89
Hankins, Mrs. J. H.
Bartlesville, OK _____ 40
Hardwick, Gail Diane
Houston, TX _____ 30, 35
Harned, Helene
Zionsville, PA _____ 173
Harrison, Clive
New York City, NY _____ 28
Harrold, Rosalind
Bainbridge, GA _____ 82
Hawley, Alice
Warner Robins, GA _____ 10, 92
Hawley, Bert
Warner Robins, GA _____ 9
Henry, Alice
Fayetteville, NY _____ 98
Herold, Donna Lee
Los Osos, CA _____ 166
Hevberger, Barbara
Wilmington, DE _____ 133
Hitch, Rhonda
Kathleen, GA _____ 131, 132
Holland, Shirley
Wallingford, PA _____ 41
Holm, Corrinne
Crystal Falls, MI _____ 70
Holmber, Bette M.
Portsmouth, RI _____ 69

Holsapple, Gay S.
  Bartlesville, OK _____ 26
Horr, Paula M.
  Moorestown, NJ _____ 119
Hudock, Lucy M.
  Riverside, CT _____ 14, 154
Hughes, Marie P.
  Berlin, NH _____ 112
Hummon, Jan
  Farmington Hill, MI _____ 156
Hyatt, Carolyn
  Santa Cruz, CA _____ 187

I

Immink, Mary Win
  Suttons Bay, MI _____ 116
Inlow, Joan H.
  Shelbyville, IA _____ 118

J

Jaffe, Frances
  Rockville, MD _____ 109
Jenkins, Eyvonne
  Escondido, CA _____ 184
Jennings, Donna
  Hawley, PA _____ 160
Johnson, Catherine
  Plains, MT _____ 148
Johnson, Ethel
  Brookline, MA _____ 87
Jones, Flo
  Royersford, PA _____ 76
Jones, Joan
  Marshall, TX _____ 128
Jones, Norma E.
  Decatur, IL _____ 97
Jubitz, Georgia
  Hood River, OR _____ 100

K

Karmirski, Janet
  Milwaukee, WI _____ 48
Keeley, Helen E.
  Phoenix, AZ _____ 154
Kelk, Ann
  Jamestown, NC _____ 136
Keller, Mrs. George E.
  South Bend, IN _____ 153
Kharasch, Robert N.
  Washington, DC _____ 183
Kiertscher, Patricia
  Downers Grove, IL _____ 57
King, Betty
  Washington, DC _____ 53
Kinney, Elizabeth H.
  Newton, NJ _____ 172

Kitchens, Betty Jean
  Dadeville, AL _____ 65
Kittredge, Ann M. C.
  Tremonton, UT _____ 126, 170
Klein, Susan
  Secaucers, NJ _____ 134
Klene, Sophie
  Arlington Heights, IL _____ 121
Knight, Carol
  Halifax, PA _____ 95
Kremen, Dr. Arnold J.
  Minneapolis, MN _____ 11

L

Labun, Lorraine G.
  Agawam, MA _____ 150
LaMar, Ronald F.
  Bettendorf, IA _____ 32
Lamb, Lori Anne
  Slaton, TX _____ 162
Langston, Shirley
  Bessemer, AL _____ 26
Lanthrip, Mrs. Bessie S.
  Mechanicsville, VA _____ 175
Larsen, Lois E.
  Las Vegas, NV _____ 161
Larsgaarp, Helen
  Hoyt Lakes, MN _____ 82
Larson, Rebecca
  Viroqua, WI _____ 31
Leavitt, Charmaine
  Kalamazoo, MI _____ 128
Lentz, Nancy
  Findlay, OH _____ 142
Lepisko, Janice
  Brownsville, VT _____ 90
Letsch, Sherry
  Glendale, AZ _____ 96
Lewis, Judy
  Gaithersburg, MD _____ 66
Lidbeck, Adrienne
  Chatham, MA _____ 18
Lind, Peter
  Novato, CA _____ 72
Lombardi, J. Richard
  San Leandro, CA _____ 59
Long, Jacquelyne P.
  Newark, DE _____ 15
Longfield, Laurie B.
  Aspen, CO _____ 129
Lordi, Helen
  Baldwin Park, CA _____ 155
Lowande, Louise M.
  North Plainfield, NJ _____ 133
Lowe, June
  Round Pond, ME _____ 72
Lowell, Edna
  El Cajon, CA _____ 150

Lucas, Phyllis A.
  Brookhaven, PA _____ 123

M

MacArthur, Mrs. Neill W.
  Jasper, GA _____ 86
Mahard, Mrs. Ada
  Natick, MA _____ 180
Margaret, Kloster
  Visalia, CA _____ 140
Martin, Janet W.
  Prescott, AZ _____ 88
Martin, Robert P.
  Indiana, PA _____ 51
Matrin, Carol L.
  Detriot, MI _____ 119
McClennen, Winnie
  Sellersville, PA _____ 97
McCoy, Darlene
  Cleveland, OH _____ 167
McDonald, Joyce
  Upper Marlboro, MD _____ 46
McGuire, Beverly
  Hollywood, CA _____ 110, 173
McKelvey, Nancy
  Williamsburg, VA _____ 176
McMahon, Mrs. George W.
  Shadyside, OH _____ 143
McNees, Janice
  Sun Valley, CA _____ 24
McQuade, Pad
  Valley Stream, NY _____ 55
Meunier, Bernard E.
  Cumberland, RI _____ 64
Mills, James
  Denver, CO _____ 116
Mistr, Donna
  Jarrettsville, MD _____ 174
Mitchell, Helen H.
  Seattle, WA _____ 61
Morgan, Dorothy B.
  Oakmont, PA _____ 76
Morris, Jay F.
  Adelphia, MD _____ 175
Morrow, Elizabeth
  Woodland Hills, CA _____ 25
Muench, Betty,
  Carefree, AZ _____ 84
Murray, Judith N.
  Bethesda, MD _____ 71
Mussari, Beverly
  Cincinnati, OH _____ 24, 29, 43, 56, 112

N

Nash, Edith
  Wisconsin Rapids, WI _____ 179

National Onion Association
  Greely, CO _____ 182, 183
Ness, Cheryl Van
  Marietta, GA _____ 85
Noonan, Joseph & Mary
  Norfolk, MA _____ 74, 151
Nordenschild, Frances
  Cranbury, NJ _____ 39
Nuttall, Mrs. Arthur Jr.
  Seneca, SC _____ 33

O

Ober, John David
  Brunswick, ME _____ 100
Ogburn, Mrs. Tilman
  Alexander City, AL _____ 162
Oller, Mrs. James E. Jr.
  Mooleyville, KY _____ 107
Onge, Barbara St.
  Haverhill, MA _____ 190
Ours, Maxine
  Butler, MO _____ 74, 160

P

Parris, Dody
  Easton, MD _____ 117
Partridge, Elizabeth
  Newport Beach, CA _____ 20
Passano, Mary F.
  Baltimore, MD _____ 114
Patten, Elizabeth
  Elbridge, NY _____ 88
Patterson, Mrs. E. A.
  Bloomsburg, PA _____ 59
Peacock, Mrs. Clarence
  Nashville, TN _____ 93
Perry, Eleanor
  New York, NY _____ 108
Pharis, Mrs. Burt
  Newmark, OH _____ 163
Phelps, Carrie
  Hillsboro, NH _____ 21
Phillips, Barbara C.
  Falls Church, VA _____ 53
Phinney, Barbara
  Sandpoint, ID _____ 33
Pirro, Mrs. Angie
  East Norwalk, CT _____ 95
Pleasants, Mrs. L. P. Jr.
  Mablehead Neck, MA _____ 184
Polin, Stephen
  Yardley, PA _____ 55
Popko, Monica
  Carrollton, TX _____ 80
Pratnicki, Marylee
  Long Branch, NJ _____ 52, 169

Prodonovich, Leslie
   Saugus, CA _____ 66
Pronko, Mrs. Michael J.
   Dalhart, TX _____ 164

R

Ramel, Mrs. George R.
   Hopkinton, OH _____ 101
Rank, Martha Gene
   Arlington, TX _____ 27
Ranneberger, Doris W.
   Bel Air, MD _____ 111
Raynolds, Patricia
   Woodstock, VT _____ 124
Reber, Albert J.
   Lakeville, MN _____ 146
Reid, Debra
   Carlisle, PA _____ 174
Repshire, Kay
   Russell Springs, KS _____ 87
Richardson, Helen G.
   Decatur, GA _____ 103
Roberts, Betty
   Maywood, NJ _____ 67
Robinson, Mrs. Wm. J.
   Hollywood, FL _____ 118
Roe, Katherine H.
   Boynton Beach, FL _____ 59
Rogers, Mrs. Joel A.
   Wickenburg, AZ _____ 13
Rosner, Lora Lee
   Cheyenne, WY _____ 156
Ross, Virginia R.
   Shrewsbury, MA _____ 176
Rowe, Thorneta
   Boyne City, MI _____ 69
Russo, Mary V.
   Rutherford, NJ _____ 13

S

Sampler, Bonnie
   Richardson, TX _____ 101
Santare, Anthony M.
   Alameda, CA _____ 189
Sasser, Mrs. Sterling
   Austin, TX _____ 75
Sauer, Joan Casson
   Locust Valley, NY _____ 146
Schlape, Helga
   Florham Park, NJ _____ 167
Schlottman, Claudia
   Macon, GA _____ 70
Schneider, M&M T.
   Mahwah, NJ _____ 158
Schultheis, Edward R.
   Massapequa, NY _____ 122

Schumacher, Anne W.
   Augusta, ME _____ 83
Schwyhart, Mrs. I. W.
   Cedarville, CA _____ 78
Selak, Carol S.
   York, PA _____ 17
Seybolt, Arlene
   Miami, OK _____ 94
Sharpsteen, Jeanette
   Palos Verdes Estates, CA _____ 165
Shoemaker, Robin C.
   Brigantine, NJ _____ 114
Shook, Mary Burney
   Raleigh, NC _____ 109, 122
Shuping, Mrs. James
   Phoenix, AZ _____ 35
Shutt, Ernestine J.
   San Jose, CA _____ 48
Sliva, Karen
   Tewksbury, MA _____ 126
Smith, Lynn
   San Diego, CA _____ 138
Snow, Robert R.
   Annandale, VA _____ 177
Spaeth, Mali E.
   Flushing, NY _____ 141
Sparks, Mrs. Don
   Lakeland, FL _____ 12
Staples, Betty P.
   Ogunquit, ME _____ 111
Staylor, Mrs. H. C.
   Princess Anne, MD _____ 59
Stewart, Linda
   Wellington, KS _____ 108
Stiewing, Alice
   Waterbury, CT _____ 155
Stine, Anne
   Shermansdale, PA _____ 95
Stokes, Bessie M.
   Sun City, AZ _____ 152
Strating, Virginia
   Fulton, IL _____ 31, 86
Stratton, Ivah D.
   Brockport, NY _____ 21
Strohm, Terry
   Woodstock, IL _____ 15
Sturgeon, June
   Medford, MA _____ 59
Sullivan, Marian
   Oshkosh, WI _____ 175
Summers, Sherry
   Pasadena, TX _____ 124
Sutton, June
   Watertown, CT _____ 36

T

Tarbell, Jennie A.
  Suffern, NY _____ 65
Taylor, Helen A.
  Clearwater, FL _____ 168
Taylor, Martha
  Maumee, OH _____ 50
Tetreault, Clair F.
  Lincoln, MA _____ 61
Tindall, Jody
  Frankfort, IN _____ 54, 91
Tischenkel, Jay M.
  Beech Mountain, NC _____ 42
Toma, Florence M.
  Port Chester, NY _____ 94
Toombs, Mrs. James
  Raye Hawthorne, NJ _____ 15
Townsend, Mrs. Rodman
  Knoxville, TN _____ 185

V

Vaida, Cynthia
  Stanton, NJ _____ 149
Valentine, Elva L.
  Whittier, CA _____ 20
Valuk, Ann M.
  Rochester, NY _____ 115
VanHees, Julia L.
  Long Beach, CA _____ 52
Vannice, Evelyn
  Grants Pass, OR _____ 66
Vitagliano, Robert
  Niagara Falls, NY _____ 143
Voris, Mrs. Milo Van
  Tucson, AZ _____ 16
Vosteen, Mabelle
  Relion, PA _____ 166

W

Wagner, Holly
  Wheaton, IL _____ 37

Walsh, Mary Terese
  Chicago, IL _____ 83
Warr, Sara Nelle
  East Ellijay, GA _____ 181
Waters, II, Mrs. G Dana
  Birmingham, AL _____ 147
Weidman, James H.
  Huntingtown, MD _____ 170
Welch, Martha
  Oakman, AL _____ 72
Wentworth, Eva R.
  Bozrah, CT _____ 78
White, Don
  Aurora, CO _____ 59
Williams, C. W.
  Englishtown, NJ _____ 99
Wilson, Linda
  Denison, TX _____ 117
Wilson, Mrs. Logan D.
  Greenville, TX _____ 104
Wongus, Elba
  Vienna, VA _____ 121
Woodward, Betty
  Fairfax, VA _____ 157
Wright, Frances
  Hemet, CA _____ 172
Wyrill, Jean
  Kirivin, KS _____ 30

Y

Yann, Mrs. Arthur A. Jr.
  Pittsburgh, PA _____ 34

Z

Zelensky, Mary C.
  Burlington, NJ _____ 125
Zizzi, Laura A.
  East Aurora, NY _____ 107

If you would like to order another copy of *"Vidalia Sweet Onion Lover's Cookbook,"* please complete this form and send to: **Bland Farms**; P.O. Box 506-630; Glennville, GA 30427

Name _____

Address _____

City _____ State_____ Zip_____

☐ *Please send this cookbook as a gift to:*

Name _____

Address _____

City _____ State_____ Zip_____

Greeting _____

Please send _____*Vidalia Sweet Onion Lover's Cookbook* ($15.95) $ _____

Postage & Handling ($3.45 each) $ _____

GA Residents add 6% sales tax $ _____

☐ *Check if you would like to receive a free catalog*   TOTAL $ _____

If you would like to order another copy of *"Vidalia Sweet Onion Lover's Cookbook,"* please complete this form and send to: **Bland Farms**; P.O. Box 506-630; Glennville, GA 30427

Name _____

Address _____

City _____ State_____ Zip_____

☐ *Please send this cookbook as a gift to:*

Name _____

Address _____

City _____ State_____ Zip_____

Greeting _____

Please send _____*Vidalia Sweet Onion Lover's Cookbook* ($15.95) $ _____

Postage & Handling ($3.45 each) $ _____

GA Residents add 6% sales tax $ _____

☐ *Check if you would like to receive a free catalog*   TOTAL $ _____

If you would like to order another copy of *"Vidalia Sweet Onion Lover's Cookbook,"* please complete this form and send to: **Bland Farms**; P.O. Box 506-630; Glennville, GA 30427

Name _____

Address _____

City _____ State_____ Zip_____

☐ *Please send this cookbook as a gift to:*

Name _____

Address _____

City _____ State_____ Zip_____

Greeting _____

Please send _____*Vidalia Sweet Onion Lover's Cookbook* ($15.95) $ _____

Postage & Handling ($3.45 each) $ _____

GA Residents add 6% sales tax $ _____

☐ *Check if you would like to receive a free catalog*   TOTAL $ _____

Please list any friends who would enjoy receiving a Bland Farms catalog or cookbook.

Name _____ Phone_____
Address _____
City_____ State_____ Zip Code_____

Name _____ Phone_____
Address _____
City_____ State_____ Zip Code_____

Name _____ Phone_____
Address _____
City_____ State_____ Zip Code_____

Please list any friends who would enjoy receiving a Bland Farms catalog or cookbook.

Name _____ Phone_____
Address _____
City_____ State_____ Zip Code_____

Name _____ Phone_____
Address _____
City_____ State_____ Zip Code_____

Name _____ Phone_____
Address _____
City_____ State_____ Zip Code_____

Please list any friends who would enjoy receiving a Bland Farms catalog or cookbook.

Name _____ Phone_____
Address _____
City_____ State_____ Zip Code_____

Name _____ Phone_____
Address _____
City_____ State_____ Zip Code_____

Name _____ Phone_____
Address _____
City_____ State_____ Zip Code_____